Making BEER

From Homebrewing to the House of Fermentology

Making BEER

From Homebrewing to the House of Fermentology

Bill Mares and Todd Haire

Illustrations by Jeff Danziger

To Tim and Nick,
the next generation of beer lovers
— B.M.

To Monica, for being so supportive
of my brewing ventures
— T.H.

Contents

Preface

Between us, Todd Haire and I have sixty years of brewing experience.

For me, it has all been in homebrewing. The evolution of my hobby began forty years ago, when there was no such thing as craft brewing and homebrewing itself was still prohibited (until President Jimmy Carter made it legal in 1978). I chronicled the adventures and misadventures of this personal journey in the first two editions of this book.

By the time Todd and I met, he had been a professional brewer working at his craft fifty to sixty hours a week for twenty years. For Todd, his first months at Hoboken Brewing in the mid-nineties hooked him on being his own boss in a brewery some day. Many years after the first success of *Making Beer* and while Todd was working at Magic Hat Brewery, he and I became friends through a shared interest in beekeeping. We brewed our first beer together in 2000, when Todd used some of my honey in a braggot beer at Magic Hat. Our friendship soon deepened, and as magically as the workings of yeast, Todd and I decided to combine our sixty years of know-how and venture forth into commercial realms together on a project to make wild beers—a style whose time is coming.

For me, going from the first two editions of *Making Beer* to opening a wild beer blendery in the bay of a local auto body shop has been like going from journalism into politics, from observation into action. For Todd, it is the logical extension of his chosen and enduring career. And it is a fitting way to close out the evolution of our journey—recounting the ascent from homebrew in the basement to professional blending in a garage.

— *Bill Mares*

❧ 1 ❧

A Fateful Glass of Homebrew

My homebrewing really began with a bagpipe lesson. Knowing of my delight in pipe music, my father bought a used set of pipes in England for my college graduation present. For the next few weeks, I made desultory attempts to learn the fingering and play simple tunes on the chanter. I couldn't get a squeak out of the pipes themselves, though, and I soon gave up.

Not until ten years later, when Chris and I moved to Vermont and hired a piper to play at our wedding, did I feel the urge to try the pipes again. Our house was far enough out in the country so that the pagan wailings were but antiphonal to the dogs' and coyotes' howling, but it was obvious that I needed help. After a few inquiries, I learned of a Scott Hastings (surely a promising name), a museum curator and piper who performed around the state.

At his home in Taftsville, Hastings looked over my pipes, took them under his arm, and tuned them for five minutes. Then he made the room reverberate with primitive, spine-tingling melodies. "These pipes are okay," he said, "but they won't play themselves, you know. You have to work at it every day."

As we prepared to leave, he asked almost in passing, "Would you like to try a homebrewed beer?"

At that, his wife, Elsie, suddenly came into focus. While we had been intent on the music, she had been working at the sink, washing out several dozen brown beer bottles. On a chair nearby sat a green garbage can covered with a piece of cheesecloth. Elsie made four or five five-gallon (two-case) batches of homebrew each year, and this was bottling day for the latest batch.

1

Scott disappeared into the basement and returned with a quart bottle. When he pried off the cap, the gentle hiss was barely audible. He poured the contents into three glasses until the last portion turned cloudy. It looked like regular beer with its clear, golden color and white, foamy head. It smelled something like beer, mixed with a tinge of cider. I took a sip. It didn't taste exactly like beer. It was both fuller and sharper than the brands I was used to drinking. It had a strong but pleasant aftertaste, sharp, but not bitter, quite pleasant.

My only prior exposure to homebrew had been secondhand. Like millions of Americans, my father had made homebrew during Prohibition. He told me of an experience which was probably repeated thousands of times during those thirteen years of national hypocrisy. He was living in Akron, Ohio, where he worked as a chemist for Goodyear Tire and Rubber Co. He did his brewing in the bathroom and then stored the beer in a closet of his second-floor apartment.

One hot summer's afternoon, the landlady called him at work to say that his beer was exploding and some of it had already leaked through the floor of his apartment. By the time he got home, most of the bottles had burst, the landlady's couch was soaked, and her mood was dark indeed. If he paid for the repairs and cleaning, and promised not to brew again, he could stay. He complied.

It is hard to grow up in Texas without drinking a lot of beer. On the Gulf Coast, where I lived, humid ninety degree weather was possible nine to ten months of the year. In contrast to Vermont, which has "eleven months of winter and one month of damned poor sledding," Texas has ten months of summer and two months of spent "northers," which bring ducks and a touch of frost. In consequence, I always seemed to be thirsty. For Texans, beer is the liquid complement to seafood, barbecue, fried chicken, and, most of all, Mexican food. Like all my friends, I was no beer connoisseur. My favorites were Bud, Miller, and Busch. I scorned regional beers like Lone Star, Pearl, Jax, and Shiner.

I applied to Harvard in part because of Guinness Stout. When I went east to visit colleges in my senior year, my brother, then at Harvard, took me to Cronin's, a popular saloon off Harvard Square. Amid the smoke, vivacious conversation, tweed jackets, and crossed rowing oars, he treated me to my first creamy, black, bittersweet Guinness. Now, this was the college life for me: study all day and drink Guinness into the night.

In Texas I learned to drink beer; at Harvard I learned to hold and appreciate it. On four of the first six Saturdays of my freshman year, I got drunk. I was not lonely, I was not depressed, but no one in the dorm seemed to know any girls, and our way of having fun was to drink Budweiser quarts from the corner liquor store. We varied the routine once or twice by holding contests to see who could down a twelve-ounce can the fastest. The time I won, I did it in 2.3 seconds by cutting two holes in one side of the can and one hole in the other.

But the prizes and wages of our beer blasts were so much retching and wretchedness that I came to hate Sundays and thus moderated my drinking. In those days, regular beer was American. There might have been some differences between Budweiser, Miller, and Schlitz, but they were lost on me.

As it turned out, I didn't drink as much Guinness as I had expected. For special occasions, perhaps twice a semester, we went to the Wursthaus, another Harvard Square watering hole that specialized in foreign beers. But they were too expensive to be dangerously habit-forming for me.

After college, when I worked in Chicago, Jimmy's Woodlawn Tap became my "local," as the English say. Jimmy's, at the corner of Fifty-fifth Street and Woodlawn Avenue, was the only building to survive a wave of urban renewal that swept through Hyde Park in the 1950s. The dirty one-story building had no sign of distinction except for the name embossed on the window. It had none of the polished oak, etched glass, or Victorian decoration that seem to grace most bars near universities.

In 1965, steins of Schlitz and hamburgers were thirty-five cents each. Bottled beer was fifty or sixty cents. Jimmy had Guinness, Bass, Tuborg, and Heineken. My favorite was Special Export from G. Heileman in Wisconsin. It had a hoppy, yet sweetish quality that set it off from the bland monotony of the national brands, and it offered the taste of imported beer at a domestic price.

Jimmy's provided the solid connection between good company and good beer. Beer was the drink of moderation and stimulating conversation. My friends did not drink beer to get drunk. If they wanted to get smashed, they went for the hard stuff.

My other favorite watering hole in Chicago (until it closed in 1967) was the Sieben Brewery, just off Armitage Avenue. Built in 1865, it was both a *Bierstube* and a beer garden. I spent many summer nights sitting in the garden downing steins of Sieben's lager. Sieben did his best to keep the brewery going, but he suffered from the competition of the majors, and the dissolution of the solid German neighborhood that had supported the brewery for so long. In the 1960s, dozens of breweries like Sieben's failed. There were just too few beer aficionados who understood that the major brands offered nothing better than Sieben's except flashier advertising.

I discovered the enormous variety and complexity of beer on travels abroad. As a member of the Harvard Glee Club, I toured the Far East, and after concerts I savored such marvels as Kirin, Asahi, Sapporo, San Miguel, Singha, and Golden Eagle. During a half-year spent studying in Germany, I drank my fill of Spaten Bräu, genuine Löwenbräu, Hacker Bräu, and seemingly dozens of local beers across Bavaria, Swabia, and the Palatinate.

Later, my work as a journalist took me to Europe and Africa. Our visit to Scott Hastings came a few months after a six-week trip to Ghana, where Chris and I consumed gallons of Club, Star, and locally made Guinness, all full-bodied and refreshing. Each time I returned to the United States, I was more disappointed with the beers offered by our big brewers. I was struck by the blandness, the icy temperature, and the hard-edged fizziness of them all.

I saw that emulating Elsie Hastings would give me a chance to avoid the big brewers. I would create my own beer at a reasonable cost and brew whatever variety I could imagine. Homebrewing fit in well with the other strains of self-sufficiency our friends were then practicing in Vermont: sheep-raising, beekeeping, vegetable gardening, and the like. That brewing was technically illegal only added to its appeal.

It was several months before I could assemble the necessary equipment from local hardware stores. I bought a ten-gallon green plastic garbage can, a capper, and a gross of caps. At a grocery store, I picked up a can of Blue Ribbon Hopped Malt Extract, five pounds of sugar, several packets of Fleischmann's baker's yeast, and some cheesecloth.

My father gave me a recipe which said to boil a gallon of water, pour in the malt syrup and sugar, boil ten to fifteen minutes, and then add four gallons of tap water to cool the brew to 80°F. Then I was to sprinkle in the yeast. I used a cross-country ski thermometer to measure that final temperature. To keep the flies out of the garbage can as the brew fermented, I draped two thicknesses of cheesecloth over the top and tied it securely. This still permitted me to watch the fermentation's progress. My father had said nothing about cleaning the bottles, so I just washed them out with soapy water, rinsed them, and let them stand.

Faithfully I followed his instructions. However, he hadn't told me that malt syrup has the consistency of 90-weight engine oil. Which meant that as I brought the liquid back to a boil, some of the undissolved syrup stuck to the bottom of the pot and burned. Undeterred, I pressed on. I assumed that since the yeast was to be added at 80°F., the ambient temperature should remain close to that, so I kept the can in front of a window where it was 75°F. during the day.

After about eight hours, a thin film had formed on the surface. The next day, the froth was about an inch deep and looked like dirty shaving cream. It did smell something like beer, though heavy on the carbon dioxide. My father said to let it perk until the head dropped and most of the bubbles disappeared, which should take four or five days.

The head eventually rose to a height of two inches, and then, as he predicted, it subsided. Or rather, collapsed. In one day it fell and disappeared. Since I could still see tiny bubbles rising to the surface, I decided to let the mixture ferment for two more days. After that, no further bubbles were evident. In their place, there appeared miniature lily pads of white moldy material about half an inch across. These were completely unexpected and didn't appear to belong in the beer, so I took a kitchen sieve and skimmed off as many as I could.

After a week, I decided it was bottling time. I carefully spooned a teaspoon of sugar into each bottle to give the beer the necessary carbonation. Then I took a length of plastic hose, held one end in the brew and put my finger over the other end. I sucked out some of the beer to create a gravity feed. It tasted a bit sharp, but not rancid. I assumed that the sugar in the bottles would even out the taste.

I managed to fill fifty bottles and only spilled a quart or so on the floor. I capped the bottles, put them in two cases, and grandly marked the boxes "HOME BREW". I carried the cases to the basement and stored them in the coolest corner.

That seemed simple enough.

About a week later, we were having breakfast when Chris asked me if I had heard a jet break the sound barrier during the night. I hadn't.

I didn't miss the second salvo.

As I was washing the dishes, there came a loud *crumpp!* from the basement, followed by the soft tinkling of glass. We didn't need some fancy problem-analysis to understand what was happening: the beer was exploding. The problem now was damage control. Should we leave the bottles there to commit suicide in peace if not quiet? They were next to the washing machine and we'd have to do a laundry sometime during the next week. Should I go down there now and cover the cases with planks of wood? That would mean that eventually all five gallons of beer would end up on the floor and shards of glass would be everywhere.

I decided I had to get the beer outside. So I bundled up in a heavy winter parka and put on Chris's ski goggles and a plastic helmet. Thick mittens and hiking boots completed my armor. While I was dressing, another bottle blew. I found a piece of half-inch plywood about the dimensions of a beer case. With this shield, I sallied down into the basement. The air was thick with the sweetish smell of spilt beer. I sneaked

around an oil tank and quickly placed my shield on top of the first case. Gently, I wiggled my fingers under it and made my way upstairs. Only then did I realize I had no protection under my chin. Another explosion might send a cap flying up through the wood to penetrate my lower jaw. Too late for such worries now.

I carried the case out to the barn and put it down in a stall. Mission half accomplished. I was sweating like a pig as I went back for the second case.

Once both cases were safely transported, I felt I just had to try one of those beers. I took an opener back to the barn. Squatting to one side, I raised the lid on a case and extracted a bottle. With its top pointed away from me, I slowly pulled off the cap. With a great hiss, white foam spewed out of the bottle. As this pocket volcano gushed forth, I took the first and last sip of my maiden batch of homebrew. It tasted like liquid, carbonated, sweetish, over-yeasty bread dough.

Back in the house, I stripped off my soaking armor. Whoever said you can't build up a thirst by 9:00 a.m. was wrong. I pulled out a Piels, popped the top with sudden respect for professional brewers, and sat down to watch the sun burn off the early-morning fog. Even as I drew my first deep swallow, another bottle exploded down in the barn.

For the next two weeks, the beer continued to lay down harassing fire, lobbing scornful shells into my enthusiasm. Perhaps, I mused, I should stick to bagpipes and bees. The former required only practice, and the stings of the latter seemed an acceptable price to pay for the sweetness of the honey.

Not an auspicious beginning for a successful homebrewer.

ஃ 2 ஃ

A Quick History of Homebrewing

In the beginning, all brew was homebrew. The exact origins of beer are unclear, but the earliest records we have of fermented beverages come from the Tigris-Euphrates valley eight thousand years before Christ was born.

No one knows when the first Sumerian peasant happened upon the idea of soaking hard barley kernels in water to soften them for eating. Similarly, no one can tell when the next peasant in that apostolic succession of homebrewers deliberately or inadvertently left some of those soaked grains to dry, chewed on them, and discovered a delightful nutty and slightly sweet flavor. And, finally, it is not clear when the next peasant ground those grains for bread and found that when soaked in water for several days the bread magically transformed the water into something not only drinkable but transporting.

Cuneiform records document brewing in Mesopotamia by 6000 BC using a variety of barleys and wheats. In time, about 40 percent of the Sumerian barley crop was devoted to beer production, and wages and salaries were often paid partly in beer.

The priesthood soon realized that people were reaching an altered state of consciousness by drinking beer, so they made haste to sanctify the potion and give it its own goddess, Ninkasi, "the lady who fills the mouth." At the same time, commercial breweries sprang up to slake the thirst of those who could not brew their own.

In his book *The Sumerians*, Samuel N. Kramer writes of Ninkasi: "Although she was a goddess, born in sparkling-fresh water," it was beer that was her first love. She is described in a hymn of glorification addressed to her by one of the devotees of the Inanna cult as the brewer of the gods who "bakes with lofty shovel the sprouted barley; who mixes the happir-malt with sweet aromatics; who bakes the happir-malt in the lofty bin; and who pours the fragrant beer in the lahtan-vessel which is like the Tigris and Euphrates joined."

In the year 2500 BC, one cuneiform text contained a long list of different words for beer, including dark beer, whitish kuran-beer, reddish beer, excellent beer, beer (mixed) of two parts, beer from the "Nether-World," beer with a head, beer which has been diluted, beer which has been clarified, beer for the sacrifice, and beer for the main (divine) repast.

Meanwhile, the art of brewing was also developing in Egypt. There, beer was looked upon as a gift of the god Osiris and was an integral part of festivals and ceremonies. In Egypt, beermaking grew directly out of breadmaking. A dough of sprouted, ground grains was partly baked, then torn apart and soaked in water for a day or two, during which time (we now know) fermentation by wild yeasts occurred. The "liquor" was strained off and the beer was ready to drink. Of course, no one knew what yeast was or how it acted on the grain sugars; but in time, brewers realized that when some of the lees of previous batches were added to a new one, the fermentation went faster.

These ancient brewers were not content with the same brew week in and week out. They experimented constantly with different flavors, spices (such as ginger and juniper) and herbs to vary the taste. With the priesthood involved, these "experiments" had strong religious and magical overtones. Beer became the national drink of Egypt. To give a party was to "arrange a house of beer."

Early brewers doubtless had plenty of failures, given the unscientific nature of the process. The Egyptians passed their brewing knowledge on to the Greeks, who in turn carried the brews to the Romans, although both those northern Mediterranean peoples preferred wine.

Meanwhile, the tribes roaming northern Europe were settling down long enough to learn to make beer using native grains, honey, and, later, barley. As early as 2000 BC the "beaker people" were producing and selling beer. Early Danes brewed a cross between wine and beer with barley, cranberries, and bog myrtle. The Roman historian, Tacitus, wrote of Germans who drank a barley-wheat beer spiced with ginger, anise, or juniper.

In medieval England, most large households had their own brewing operations. The beers varied in strength from the equivalent of near beer to strong barley wines. The northern European peasantry generally drank large quantities of low-alcohol beer in the same manner and for the same reason that nineteenth-century New England farmers consumed hard cider—it was safer than the water.

Hops, the viny source of modern beer's pleasant bitterness, was only one of many flavors added to beer until the eighth or ninth century AD. After that, there are records of the continuous use of hops in Bavarian beer. By the end of the fifteenth century, hops had become barley's inseparable partner in most Continental beers.

The introduction of hops into England, however, caused a furor. Lovers of unhopped ale fought a rearguard action against the Dutch hops that had gained a foothold of cultivation in Kent. In fact, Henry VIII banned their importation, but by the end of the sixteenth century, the English marriage of hops and barley malt was generally accepted.

Thus the term *ale*, which originally distinguished English beer from hopped Continental beer, came to mean top-fermented (and hopped) English-style brew in contrast to the bottom-fermented (lager) variety. Hopped beer seems to have won the day because of its excellent preservative and sterilizing qualities in addition to its ability to balance the malt. (In the rest of this book, I have adopted the English custom of referring to both beer and ale as "beer." When Shakespeare wrote, "I will make it felony to drink small beer," he meant ale. When I say "ale," I will mean the top-fermented beer.)

The first white settlers in North America brought with them both commercial and homebrewing. The Jamestown colony made a poor beer out of Indian corn. The Pilgrims at Plymouth, according to the diary of one of their members, were in distress because they "could not now take time for further search or consideration, our victuals being much spent, especially Beere."

John Alden, a cooper by trade and caretaker of the *Mayflower*'s beer barrels, decided to settle in the new land with the immigrants when he saw their need for beer.

Beer was a staple of the Puritans' diet, as attested by this passage from the diary of minister Richard Mather in 1635: "And a speciall means of ye healthfulnesse of ye passengers by ye blessing of God wee all conceyved to bee much walking in ye open ayre, and ye comfortable variety of our food; . . . we had no want of good and wholesome beere and bread."

In 1630, the year my mother's ancestors came to America from England, one ship, the *Arbella*, left port carrying three times as much beer as water.

Pastors and public officials praised the benefits of beer because it provided a stout defense against the ravages of "strong waters," a euphemism for Demon Rum.

In 1635, within six years of the establishment of the West India Company colony on Manhattan, its Dutch inhabitants had built their first brewery. English and Dutch brewers and homebrewers had to weigh the expense and time of securing ingredients from Europe against the search for local sources of supply. The wealthy continued to import beer from Europe, but anyone living even a few miles from the port cities soon turned to his own devices. Homebrewing was not a hobby but a necessity.

The colonists used wild hops when they could find them, or substituted ground ivy and juniper berries. One of the most popular alternatives was essence of red or black spruce, which also worked well as a preventative against scurvy.

If barley be wanting to make into malt
We must be content and think it no fault
For we can make liquor to sweeten our lips
Of pumpkins, and parsnips, and walnut-tree chips.

As Mark E. Lender, a modern writer on American drinking habits, has put it: "One suspects that the beers produced from such recipes were little better than the poetry."

Like their English forebears, early American settlers brewed roughly three classes of beer, according to strength. The weakest and most commonly drunk was called small beer. At the other end of the spectrum was strong beer, so defined by the length of time the malt was soaked in water to convert starches into fermentable sugars. Strong beer, which might have 6 to 7 percent alcohol, was a favorite of the wealthier classes, who could usually afford an in-house brewer. In between was middle beer, or table beer.

All these beers were cloudy, an aesthetic fact traceable to the top-fermenting yeast which had evolved in England. One reason for the popularity of hard cider among the colonial elite was that, in contrast to beers of all strengths, the cider was clear. As beer historian Stanley Baron wrote in *Brewed in America*: "The most characteristic aspect of brewing in the seventeenth century, however, was its chanciness. Brewers understood very little about the technology of their trade, and the chemistry involved was a total blank to them. Even measuring devices, such as the thermometer, the hydrometer. . . and the attemperator ... did not come into practical use until the second half of the eighteenth century. Everything about their brewing was inaccurate and capricious; they could not explain why one brew came out well and the next poorly. The properties and control of yeast remained unexplored until the researches of Pasteur and Hansen in the 1870s. No wonder we find references to 'the art and *mystery* of brewing.' "

Baron suggests that one of the first recorded recipes for homebrewing in North America was written down by George Washington:

To Make Small Beer

Take a large Siffer [Sifter] full of Bran Hops to your Taste. Boil these 3 hours then strain out 30 Gallons into a Cooler put in 3 Gallons Molasses while the Beer is Scalding hot or rather draw the Molasses into the Cooler & St[r]ain the Beer on it while boiling Hot. Let this stand till it is little more than Blood warm then put in a quart of Yea[s]t if the Weather is very Cold cover it over with a Blank[et] & let it Work in the Cooler 24 hours then put it into the Cask—leave the Bung [Stopper] open till it is almost don[e] Working—Bottle it that day Week it was Brewed.

In his retirement, the polymath Thomas Jefferson turned to brewing with characteristic thoroughness. Baron quotes his answer to an inquiry about private brewing from James Madison:

Our brewing for the use of the present year has been some time over. About the last of Oct. or beginning of Nov. we begin for the ensuing year, and malt and brew three sixty gallon casks ... in as much as you will want a house of Malting, which is quickest made by digging into the steep side of a hill, so as to need a roof only, and you will want a hair cloth also of the size of your loft to lay the grain in. This can only be had from Philadelphia or New York. ... I will give you notice in the fall when we are to commence malting and our malter and brewer is uncommonly intelligent and capable of giving instruction if your pupil is as ready at comprehending it.

The differences in technique between homebrewing and commercial brewing were not great, even into the nineteenth century. Until Pasteur's isolation of yeast culture, both had to rely upon the careful extraction and retention of the lees in which rested the yeast from the previous batch.

By the beginning of the nineteenth century, there were some 132 breweries in the United States, producing 285,000 barrels annually. (In the same year, a single London brewery, The Anchor, made 205,000 barrels.)

In 1840, a Philadelphia brewer named John Wagner brought some bottom-fermenting yeast from Germany to his small establishment on

St. John Street. There, in a kettle hung over an open hearth, he brewed eight barrels of beer, which were subsequently stored (lagered) in the cellar. (*Lagern* in German means "to store.") From these humble beginnings arose a tidal wave of lager beer, which by 1880 had engulfed the country.

Before 1840, all beers drunk in the United States were top-fermented ales, porters, and stouts. After 1880, over 90 percent of the beer was bottom-fermented lager. There were several reasons for the switch. First, the highly carbonated lager was more thirst-quenching in the hotter climate of the United States. Second, it was clearer and its introduction coincided with the invention of cheap, transparent glass in which to serve the beer. Third, the failed German revolution of 1848 sent thousands of discontented emigrants to the New World. Some of them were brewers, and almost all were lager drinkers. Germans set up hundreds of local and regional breweries in the following years. So ubiquitous were these breweries, and so good were their products, that fewer and fewer people bothered to brew their own. One authority on the history of American food, Richard J. Hooker, also suggests that lighter-bodied lagers were more compatible with Americans' relatively high-meat diet.

The need for refrigeration in both the manufacture and storage of lager made it next to impossible for homebrewers to match the store-bought or saloon beer. Homebrewing became the province of a few cranks and those isolated on the frontier. People who lived scores of miles from the nearest brewery used recipes not unlike this one from the Australian outback, courtesy of Ian McDonald:

4 lbs. white sugar
1 tsp. dry baker's yeast
1 lb. brown sugar
2 lbs. Saunders Malt extract
3 oz. hops
2 gals. water
1 tsp. salt

Boil 1 gal. of water in enamel bucket, add hops tied in bag and make it sit down and soak. Boil 20 minutes, take bag out. squeeze out as soon as cool and put back into brew. While bag is cooling, add all other ingredients except yeast. When everything has dissolved, add the other gallon of water. Stick finger in at blood heat, add yeast at this temperature.

Put bucket in warmest place, possibly a cupboard, and cover with a towel to let air in. Don't move around.

Skim off froth and flies. Leave approximately 7 days in warm place, until top clears and sediment drops. Siphon into another container, anything, wash out sediment, and pour back into bucket. Leave another 24 hours to settle again. Siphon again and then bottle one-third full. Top up with clean water.

Soak bottle tops in water beforehand to wet cork for one half hour. Cap the bottles. Store bottles standing up in a cool place. Start drinking after a fortnight—preferably a month. Must be cold.

Homebrewing returned to the United States under duress. On January 16, 1920, Prohibition became law and millions of citizens like my father became lawbreakers. Offended equally by the law and by bootleggers' prices, would-be brewers had to start from scratch. There were no recipe books and certainly no homebrew supply shops selling ingredients and equipment. Most homebrewers had to rely upon the imperfect and often foggy memories of their own fathers.

Their chief inspiration was Lena, the round and warm-faced woman who graced the label of the Blue Ribbon malt can manufactured by Pabst. Fortunately, malt could still be sold because of its use in baking.

When homebrewers couldn't find Lena, they resorted to all kinds of alternatives, such as corn, rice, and wheat. By and large, the result was powerful, cidery, cloudy, and tolerable only because of the alcohol it contained.

Joseph De Benedetti, part owner of a homebrew supply store in

Portland, Oregon, described his Prohibition brewing:

> "We would take a carton of malt, three pounds of sugar and a package of Fleischmann's cake yeast. We used stone jars—six gallons for a five-gallon batch and twelve gallons for a ten-gallon batch. It usually fermented for one week in the crock. Sometimes you'd put light bulbs around it to force it, but if you had a cool basement and it fermented slowly, it made a better beer.
>
> "We'd use two and a half pounds of malt. Bring your water to a rolling boil, put your hops in, and bring it down to a simmer for about twenty minutes. That would be the best brew. When it cooled down a little bit, you added your yeast and it would foam up in the first day or two. You could skim that off, but it wasn't necessary. You boiled the whole batch at once. Lots of people couldn't be bothered to boil: they'd just mix it up. Then, depending on your patience, it would be about two weeks before you drank it. Sometimes it was good, most of the time it was terrible. I always had pretty good luck.
>
> "Everybody claimed they made the best beer in town. They would make it so darn strong—they would double up on the malt, and the sugar would all ferment out. They would get a high hydrometer reading, but it wouldn't all turn into alcohol because the yeast can only eat so much sugar. You'd have to give it a second shot of yeast. You would have to have the right temperature—sixty to seventy degrees. It was called a warm fermentation."

Beer drinkers came out of Prohibition with both an enormous thirst and a violent distaste for homebrew. The commercial breweries were more than happy to welcome them back with a clear, predictable, inoffensive beer that didn't bite. Drinkers were in no mood to talk about the fine points of beer: they wanted to know and see what they were drinking, and they wanted to drink a lot of it.

In 1876, there were over 2,600 brewing companies in the United States. This number had fallen to 1,100 by 1919. Just over 700 breweries reopened at the end of Prohibition, fourteen years later. By 1976, fewer than fifty brewing companies remained. The reduction in numbers was matched by a similar narrowing of beer styles, as brewers formulated beers according to the lowest-common-denominator principle. In a nation bubbling with ethnic diversity, breweries opted for blandness over distinctiveness, inoffensiveness over pleasure, advertising over ingredients, and adjuncts over barley.

In the 1930s, a few regional brewers began to explore national distribution. To ship their beers from Milwaukee or St. Louis cost an extra "premium," which was added to the local distributor's price. Through the wonders of modern marketing, the brewers were able to convince the public that the premium was an indication of goodness, not a noun describing an extra cost. Hence the term *premium* beers. In actual fact, many of the local beers tasted better than the national ones, but they were overshadowed by the so-called premium brands from breweries that were also able to foot the tremendous costs of national advertising.

Another reason for the "lightening" of American beers was the marketing decision during and after World War II to appeal to women, who were thought to prefer a milder taste. The growth of the take-home market, the packaging of beer in cans, and their ready availability in supermarkets also meant that more and more the decision of which beer to buy was being made, at that time, by women.

In the 1960s, the Peter Hand Brewing Company in Chicago introduced Meister Brau Lite, and the Gablinger Brewery in New York offered a similar low-calorie beer. They sold modestly well, but were hampered by small advertising budgets. It required the resources of a cigarette maker, Philip Morris, to change the face of American beer. In 1972, Philip Morris acquired Meister Brau and its Lite label and then merged it with the already swallowed Miller Brewing Company. Using the weight and sophistication of a massive advertising campaign, Miller moved from seventh to second place among U.S. brewers (behind Anheuser-Busch) and from 5 million barrels to 31 million barrels in sales. Their slogan became "All you ever wanted in a beer. And less." It was a stunning marketing success; one which Budweiser did not take seriously until Miller Lite had already captured over 40 percent of the low-calorie market. By 1992, low-cal beers accounted for over 30 percent of total American beer sales.

Not everyone welcomed or accepted the homogenization of beer. Students, servicemen, and others who had tasted good beers abroad came home to the sameness of most American brews. The health-consciousness and do-it-yourself movements merged to spawn a breed of people who cared more about what they ate and drank and had the time to prepare that better fare. Some of them were incensed that beer and wine remained the only major food products exempt from federal ingredients-listing requirements. Finally, there were tens of thousands of people who still, quietly, made their own beer in the old-fashioned Prohibition manner, despite homebrewing's assumed illegality.

When Prohibition ended, the government specifically legalized the home manufacture and consumption of wine, up to two hundred gallons per two-person household, but it said nothing about beer. For the next forty years, therefore, the public assumed that homebrewing was still illegal, although there were no known cases of prosecution for it. Wine supply stores and a number of mail-order seed catalogues began to offer some homebrew supplies in the late 1960s and early 70s.

Some of the more enterprising and intrepid winemaking supply stores began to import English malt syrups and extracts such as John Bull, Edme, and Munton & Fison for making beer. The English malt-ing companies, having saturated their domestic markets, looked to the Americans for additional sales. They provided recipes for English ales, stouts, and porters, as well as lagers. Most homebrewers were primarily interested in making something that in any case would be clearly differ-ent from American beers.

In 1977-1978, an amalgam of California homebrewers, led by

writer Lee Coe and members of such clubs as the Redwood Lagers, the Maltose Falcons, and the San Andreas Malts, persuaded Senator Alan Cranston to sponsor a bill giving homebrewing the same legal status as winemaking. The bill was passed by both houses of Congress and signed by President Carter in 1979.

The key provision of the bill read:

> Beer for Personal or Family Use—Subject to regulation prescribed by the Secretary of the Treasury, any adult may, without payment of tax, produce beer for personal or family use and not for sale. The aggregate amount of beer exempt from tax under this subsection with respect to any household shall not exceed—(1) 200 gallons per calendar year if there are 2 or more adults in such household or (2) 100 gallons per calendar year if there is only 1 adult in such household.

Another ingredient in this beer revolution was the rising demand for imported beers. For years, Heineken led the imports, controlling as much as 40 percent of the market (as it still did in 1981). But millions of Americans were now traveling abroad and bringing home pleasant memories of dozens of other brands, including San Miguel from the Philippines, Dos Equis from Mexico, and Fischer's from France. Imported beer sales rose over 1,000 percent during the 1970s and '80s. Still, that amounted at most to 5 percent of the total U.S. beer consumption. In northern Vermont, Molson, Moosehead, and Labatt became so popular that many people didn't think of them as imports.

The American beer industry was in turmoil over style, taste, and concentration. It was bisected by seemingly conflicting trends: one group of consumers appeared to want blander, weaker, less distinctive beers—the low-calorie offerings. But another segment demanded heavier, more flavorful, fuller-bodied beers, which were now being marketed as "super-premiums," and the imports. Squeezed in the middle were the regular beers and the smaller regional breweries.

As the major brewers fought each other for a larger market share, they played corporate Pac-Man, devouring one brewery after another until it appeared as if the end of the 1980s would see what Russell Cleary, president of G. Heileman & Co., called a "duopoly"—of Anheuser-Busch and Miller.

And where were the homebrewers in all this? "Without measurable impact," according to a spokesman for the U.S. Brewers Association.

∼ 3 ∼

From Mother Earth to the Heartland and Back

I couldn't give up brewing after one try. If my bagpiping could improve, so could my beermaking. What's more, I had grandly told many friends that my beer would be better than anything they had ever tasted before. It was a way to set myself apart from the talents of fly-fishermen, carpenters, poets, and stonemasons. To quit after one attempt would be mortifying, although I was beginning to realize that brewing was not as easy as I had anticipated.

My father's advice, when he heard of my explosive failure, was to add less sugar. He pointed out that fermentation has two by-products—alcohol and carbon dioxide. The bottles probably blew up because I hadn't completed the fermentation and there was no place for the CO_2 to go.

This time I wrote down every step in my procedure, including the fact that I used two-thirds the previous amount of sugar. I also made one small methodological advance: instead of spooning out one teaspoon of sugar into each bottle, I dissolved the whole amount (about a cup) in hot water and then added the solution to the five gallons of brew just before bottling.

When this batch was bottled, I took it directly to the barn and for the next two weeks checked the cases daily. No explosions, so that was progress. I waited another week before trying some. Wearing my goggles, but not the overcoat, I retrieved one bottle. To reduce the chances of a gusher, I put it in the freezer for a couple of hours. Then I took it outside and opened it ever so slowly. A quiet, subtle *shissss* gave me hope, but the first sip dashed all expectation in a puckering bouquet of vinegar. I fetched another bottle. Same result. "Well, there's plenty

of vinegar for pickles," Chris said cheerfully. I was not amused. One by one I opened each bottle and sniffed it, hoping to find an exception. No such luck.

It was obvious that in some way this batch had become contaminated. At the town library I looked in vain for homebrewing books that might tell me what to do. Nothing. In the *Encyclopedia Britannica*, the seven pages on brewing contained an elaborate history and description of commercial brewing technology, but nothing about homebrew.

For the next batch, I cleaned the garbage can with a chlorine bleach solution, then scrubbed it with baking soda solution instead of soap and water, and topped out with a clean water rinse just before brewing. I also used the garbage can cover instead of cheesecloth, reasoning that, the more airtight I kept the fermenter, the less chance there'd be for contaminating critters to get in and spoil my beer.

At times, I felt as scientific as Lister, Jenner, or Pasteur; at other moments, like a bumbling alchemist. I had told my friends I was brewing my own beer, but whenever they asked for a sample, I said I had none left. I didn't reveal that I had thrown out both batches.

This third batch was my make-or-break effort. If it turned sour again, I would go back to beekeeping as my primary hobby. I let the batch age for a full month. Then, one day, after helping a neighboring farmer hay his fields, I was drenched in sweat and grime. What a fine opportunity to try the brew, I thought. I put two bottles in the freezer and sat down on the stoop with the farmer to talk about the coming deer season.

After ten minutes, I retrieved the bottles and casually, if carefully, pried off the caps. There was an inviting hiss. I told him that this was my first "real" effort, neglecting to mention that the others had been total failures. The brew looked clear and it had good foam. It smelled a bit yeasty but, wonder of wonders, it tasted like beer—malty, bitter, and refreshing.

In retrospect, it was probably a typically cidery Blue Ribbon homebrew. But I thought it was darned good. And so did my neighbor, at least that's what he said. It reminds me now of our first maple syrup, when we ignorantly boiled the sap down to industrial-grade darkness, or the first honey from our hives, laced with bits of bee bodies. The beer would win no prizes, but it was drinkable and it was ours. The emotional investment blotted out a host of faults.

The farmer finished the whole bottle, sediment and all. I drank another bottle. It wasn't exactly smooth, but the flavor was strong and, I thought, very European.

During the next few days, I found numerous opportunities to tell friends about my brewing success. In fact, I was about as shy and retiring as a new father. A couple of weeks later, a writer/farmer friend, Nat Tripp, invited us for dinner and suggested, "Since your beer is so good, why not bring some?"

On the night of the party, I chilled a six-pack in the freezer and then wrapped the bottles in an old blanket for the drive over the dirt roads, so we wouldn't get hurt if any exploded.

While the other guests helped themselves to gin and tonics or Budweisers, I opened a couple of my bottles. I poured out several glasses and carried them to the guests. The head disappeared in the first twenty seconds, but Nat sniffed appreciatively. "Ah, there's no smell quite like that of homebrew!"

Looking like royal servants tasting for poison, two other guests sipped the beer. They paused, their faces stiff masks of politeness. "A little young?" one queried between clenched teeth. "Five weeks," I replied. "Perhaps it needs to age a bit more." The other guinea pig said, "It's okay for homebrew," and set the glass down, never to touch it again. One lawyer friend didn't mince words: "You don't mean you prefer this to Bud?"

I laughed, but inside I was hurt. I felt as if I had just helped an elderly lady across the street and instead of thanking me she had kicked me in the shins. I drank the rest of the six-pack myself.

A week or so later, a letter arrived from Tripp. Inside was an article about homebrewing from that back-to-the-land missal, *Mother*

Earth News.

The article began with a rather mystifying editor's note:

The Justice Department of the Federal Government long ago announced that it would pursue a hands-off policy on any beer made for home consumption and not for sale. In recent years, however, the Alcohol and Tobacco Tax Division of the Treasury Department has informally attempted to enforce commercial laws on homebrewers and, thereby, discourage another time-honored, down home, do-it-yourself activity.
Lawyers say the Feds' argument would never hold up in court. Nevertheless, we do not encourage anyone to brew any beer until he is thoroughly satisfied that such activities are completely within the law and that he has complied with all applicable federal, state and local regulations.

Perhaps the editors wanted to cover their rears so the ATF (Alcohol, Tobacco, and Firearms) agents would not swoop down on their office and rummage through their stash of goat's milk and granola bars.

The article itself was decidedly schizophrenic. It delighted in accounts of "friends who experimented with ginger, cracked corn or corn meal. The results were no longer beer but a high octaine [sic] mixture similar to mead. Some of these formulas laid out respectable beer drinkers like they were school boys." On the other hand, it did stress the danger of bottling too early and recommended recording recipes so the brewer could repeat the ones he liked and, presumably, avoid repeating the failures.

Mother Earth News tossed me into the first of several briar patches of conflicting or just plain lousy advice and information. Had I a conspiratorial turn of mind, I might have believed that the writers of this and other articles were ATF agents spreading black propaganda or disinformation about the homebrewing craft as a means of suppressing it.

To its credit, the article did help me produce drinkable beer about one time out of three. I poked along for a couple of years, making about four batches a year, knowing I could drink the results even if my friends opted for Bud and Molson. Many bottles did taste like overfermented cider. When I noticed that guests tended to leave glasses of the beer untouched under chairs or to nourish the ferns with it, I realized that homebrew was not for everyone. Brewing on this level was like a low-grade addiction: I couldn't give it up, but it didn't incapacitate me.

In the mid-1970s, I worked for a newspaper across the Connecticut River in New Hampshire. It was at least a forty-five-minute drive home even on clear nights, and in snow it could take twice that long. I confess that I often drank a sixteen-ounce bottle of homebrew on that drive most nights. On particularly hot and thirsty summer evenings, I would buy one of those huge twenty-six-ounce cans of Foster's lager, which look more like oil cans than containers to hold beer.

I learned that there were more sophisticated ways to brew when I found an elementary text in a secondhand bookstore in Boston. *Home Brewing Without Failures,* by H. E. Bravery, made interesting reading but was almost useless for any practical brewing. He called for ingredients unobtainable in the U.S., like Demerara sugar and roasted malt. What's more, his recipes required such procedures as immersing a heater in the grain and water for eight hours. I just wanted to make beer, not start a brewery.

The New Hampshire newspaper fell victim to the recession, and Chris and I moved so I could take a job in Grand Rapids, Michigan. Grand Rapids remains, in my memory, a city dominated by the automobile, churches, and beer. We rented half a house across from a Dutch Reformed church that held services in English at 10:00 a.m. and in Dutch at 2:00 p.m. Our landlord next door warned us that people in Grand Rapids took the Sabbath seriously and asked us not to wash the car or mow the grass on Sunday. In his own family, even the work of cooking was not done on Sunday.

For most of that year, I was a night police reporter covering fires, highway fatalities, murders, and lesser crimes. When I went out to drink beer with my fellow reporters, I found myself more conscious of their drinking habits. Most of them consumed great quantities of "Fire-Brewed Bohemian Style" Stroh's. On all occasions, drinking was characterized by a race to fill the table with empty bottles and tell stories of past drinking bouts and hangovers. The bars seemed full of boisterous, yet lonely people. To them, beer was simply a means for getting drunk; not a drink to be savored for its taste. I didn't think of myself as some effete Eastern drinker merely recoiling from the butter-and-eggs boozers of the Midwest. I was sure it was the memory of my struggles to make decent homebrew which alienated me from these drinking bouts.

Returning one evening from covering some mayhem, I drove by a store called the Village Wine Cellar, which sold home wine- and beer-making supplies. I went back the following day, and from the moment I entered that room, redolent with the odors of hops, malt, and wine concentrates, my life and beer were never the same.

The proprietor, with the preoccupied air of an academic researcher, introduced himself as Tallmadge Nichols and invited me to browse. One side of the room was devoted to winemaking supplies—grape-crushing tubs, racking equipment, corking devices, cans of fruit concentrate, etc., all displayed under posters of sunny California or France.

It was the other side that caught my fancy: half a store containing homebrewing supplies. Back and forth, like a shopper without a list, my eyes roamed from cans of Munton & Fison malt syrup standing like Grenadier Guards, to bags of green- and brown-leaved hops. One shelf held boxes of top-fermenting and bottom-fermenting yeasts. There were bags of hops pellets with exotic names like Bullion, Cascade, and Hallertau. There were small vials of white powders labeled sodium metabisulphite, gypsum, brewing salts, and packets of a brown material that looked like seaweed (and was) but went under the name of Irish Moss. On the floor were large white plastic tubs with tight-fitting lids.

"That's food-grade plastic," Nichols said, breaking into my mental comparison with the green garbage can I used. "Sometimes you can get off-flavors from the other kinds of plastic." Coils of clear plastic hose lay nearby like a whaler's rope. There was a group of glass carboys such as I used to see in office water coolers. Atop each one was a Rube Goldberg device of stiff clear plastic. Near the cash register stood a revolving book rack with manuals and pamphlets about wine- and beermaking.

"I'm in your hands," I told Nichols. "What do I need to make good homebrew?"

Nichols led me into the back room. From a refrigerator he drew out a plain brown bottle with a silver cap, and from a shelf he retrieved a long-stemmed beer glass. After carefully opening the bottle, he poured a golden beer into the glass, apologizing that it was only a month old.

That first sip sounded the death knell for my *Mother Earth News* beer. This brew was smooth, bitter without being sour, sweet without being sugary, and well balanced. "How can I make some of this?" I asked. "Very easily," he replied. "We have a standard recipe which we give out to all first-time brewers, and they seem quite satisfied." He added that he didn't generally offer beer to someone off the street, but I seemed to be genuinely interested and not just looking for a free drink.

Nichols had started the store about ten years earlier and first concentrated on winemaking equipment. Homebrewing was then limited to Blue Ribbon malt extracts. Its technical illegality and the power of commercial beer advertising had effectively deterred manufacturers from offering a variety of homebrewing products for the American market.

In the early 1970s, when British malt manufacturers began to ship their products across the Atlantic, Nichols was one of the first retailers willing to stock them. Along with the ingredients came books by Englishmen, such as Dave Line's *Big Book of Brewing*, C. J. J. Berry's *Home Brewed Beers and Stouts,* and Ken Shales's *Advanced Home Brewing.* The language and measurements were British and a bit confusing. Then the maltmakers began to offer homebrew kits with all the ingredients for a batch at a package price. "That changed the market," Nichols observed. "What's more, they provided much better recipes and advice than had existed before."

I told Nichols how faulty I thought the *Mother Earth News* recipe was. Nichols, a man obviously not given to hyperbole, agreed it was "exceedingly bad."

"Most of my customers are more price-conscious than quality-conscious. They want it simple and easy and cheap. They don't want to make a lot of measurements." On the other hand, heavy beer drinkers did not patronize Nichols's store, because "a man who consumes one or two six-packs a night would go through a batch of homebrew in less than a week. Such people don't want to spend all their spare time brewing and bottling. In fact, those who make their own beer probably end up drinking less than when they buy it, because they have put some of themselves into the brewing."

The few customers who learned their brewing during Prohibition were convinced that nothing could improve their beer. They scorned the English malts as expensive and effete.

"Prohibition-style brewers never spend much time or take temperature readings," Nichols went on. "They put the beer in a container and start drinking it in three days whether it is in the bottle or not. They think that is the only way to make beer. They come in and want to argue that their way is the only way. I don't like to argue. Maybe I have converted a few, but if they've made it the old way, it is not likely they will change. The commonest converts to homebrewing are those who start from scratch, with no previous knowledge or prejudices."

The lager recipe Nichols gave me called for a can of Munton & Fison malt syrup, dextrose or corn sugar, and Hallertau hops pellets, whose aroma he told me was filling the room.

"You will need some more equipment than I presume you own now," he said. "A secondary fermenter, for example. That's what those carboys are for. Beer needs to ferment under completely airless and thus bacteria-free conditions. Good beer needs to be aged. The plastic device on the carboy is a fermentation lock, or bubbler, which allows the carbon dioxide to escape from the beer without admitting any airborne contaminants. You have to keep water in that bubbler," he warned. Several of his customers had neglected this requirement and wondered why their beer spoiled. "And don't boil the darn thing," he added. Another customer, in a fit of sterilizing frenzy, had done that, and the bubbler had melted into strange and unusable contortions.

Nichols's rule of thumb was to leave the beer in the primary plastic bucket for four or five days for the first bloom of fermentation to occur, then transfer it by plastic tube into the clean secondary fermenter, where it remained until the bubbles in the airlock came only every ninety seconds. Depending upon the ambient temperature, the aging could take two to four weeks. At that point, he transferred the five gallons back to the (cleaned) primary, added a cup of dextrose dissolved in hot water, and bottled it in a fashion I was familiar with. He had, however, improved upon my procedure of controlling the flow by pinching the end of the plastic tube with my fingers: he sold plastic twist valves, which reduced the mess and saved about a quart of beer.

I tried my first batch the following Sunday. The directions were simple. I mixed the malt, dextrose, and hops and boiled the lot for forty-five minutes. Then I poured the wort into the primary, freshly cleaned with baking soda and hot water, added enough tap water to make five gallons, and sprinkled the powdered yeast on those untroubled waters.

By the middle of the Dutch services that afternoon, the yeast had begun to work, for there was a telltale layer of tiny bubbles forming on the surface. I carried the forty-five pounds of bucket and liquid to the cool basement and let it perk for the next five days, allowing myself one sniff each day. The surface showed an ugly eruption of gray and brown foam, like Bluto's shaving cream. It smelled inviting, sharp, and fresh, and much hoppier than my Vermont homebrew. After five days, the foam had receded and I transferred the brew to the carboy. Like an explorer planting the flag, I attached the fermentation lock and dropped a black plastic garbage bag over the carboy to keep out the light.

I then hauled the carboy back up to the dining room and placed it in a corner. For two weeks, it sat there, a squat black sentry with a gradually less frequent hiccup: *blup, blup, blup.* By the end of the second week, the bubbles had slowed to one every ninety seconds. With Clorox, hot water, and baking soda, I cleaned out two cases of Stroh's bottles. I made up the priming sugar and poured it into the clean primary fermenter, then transferred the beer from the carboy, using a plastic tube. About a quart of yeasty sediment remained on the bottom of the carboy. The bottles I stored in the coolest corner of the basement.

For three weeks, I made impatient moves in their direction. None blew up. One night, after covering a train wreck and a homicide, I felt I really deserved a beer. I stuck one in the freezer, sat down, and waited for fifteen minutes.

When I popped the top, there wasn't much foam, but what a taste!— as good as that which Nichols had served me—smooth, good balance of hops and malt, none of that liquid bread or stiff cidery taste of Prohibition pilsner. I was so pleased that I had another bottle at cellar temperature and went to bed luxuriating in my first real success.

In the following months, I brewed several more batches, varying either the malt or the hops, but not both. Each time the beer tasted different but still good. Along the way, I made my first convert, Roger Conner, an environmental lawyer. Working sixty hours a week and rebuilding his house wasn't enough for Roger. He needed more things to do. Carpentry gave him a thirst, so homebrewing was a natural add-on. I gave him Nichols's recipe and lent him the ingredients. Fortunately, he knew how to follow directions, and his first effort was as good as my fourth.

I had no success in sharing my homebrew with my hard-drinking newspaper friends. They were not interested, and I didn't force them. I kept Stroh's and Pabst on hand for their visits and, I confess, a few bottles for myself. I knew that they and the imports were still better than my beer.

After a year in Grand Rapids, I found a newspaper job back in Vermont. By the time we left, I was making a fair "house" beer. When we packed the U-Haul for the journey home, the carboy, plastic pail, tubes, and capper were as much a part of our belongings as the dictionary, typewriter, and dog.

❧ 4 ❧

Mud Pies for Adults

My first Vermont brewing acolytes were two newspaper reporters and a photographer. We started the evening with two six-packs of the Canadian malt liquor Brador, which one reporter had brought back from a trip to Montréal. By the time we had finished boiling the wort for a Grand Rapids lager, we were pretty rowdy. (The wort is the malt-sugar-laden liquid prior to fermentation; if it has been boiled it is called "bitter" wort, as opposed to sweet.) I lost track of the measurements halfway through the brew, but I didn't think it would matter. The next morning, I realized that in my alcoholic fog I had forgotten to put in the yeast. That batch was eventually drinkable, but it had an off-taste that was no doubt related to my lack of attention.

As I brewed my batches of Nichols's lager every couple of months, my consumption of commercial beer declined steadily, although, like a new vegetarian who sneaks hamburgers, I would regress on occasion. For several years, I didn't force my beer on anyone. Twice burned, thrice shy of offending others. Even when a few people asked for it, I was a master of self-deprecation: "This isn't for everyone," I would warn. Or, "Like the moonshiner said, the only thing I guarantee is that you don't go blind."

But gradually the balance shifted in favor of my own brew. Chris would drink three or four bottles a week, and an occasional friend might enjoy a glass. When we brought some to a party, a few guests would try it. I drank at least one bottle a night. This meant that the two-case batches were being consumed at a much faster rate than before, like snow melting on a warm spring day.

I had three options: cut down on my consumption, buy more

commercial beer, or make larger amounts of my own. I chose the third alternative.

Two obstacles presented themselves. The first was that Burlington water tasted funny. The municipal water system was antiquated, having remained unchanged for seventy years. The water department was about to present a multimillion-dollar bond issue to the voters, but even if it was approved, repairs would not be completed for four years. To compensate for the failing mechanical and piping system, the city dumped more and more chlorine and other chemicals into the water, until it seemed as if you were brushing your teeth in a public swimming pool.

I needed better water. I started carrying empty gallon milk or cider jugs in the trunk of our car, and whenever we visited friends in the country I filled up with their water. This meant that I rarely used water with the same chemical balance twice, but that inconsistency didn't seem to matter in the long run.

The second obstacle was that, even as I perfected my technique for Grand Rapids lager and adopted it as my steady brew, I felt twinges of boredom. I began to thirst for some ale and stout, and some different-tasting lagers. One day, as I was looking through our bookshelves for something to read, I found the three homebrewing booklets I had bought in Grand Rapids but had never opened. I chose Byron Burch's *Guide for the Home Production of Fine Beers*.

Burch's book opened with two recipes for a light-bodied pale ale and a dark beer. They seemed pretty complex and involved. There were "flavoring" hops and "aromatic" hops added at different times. The recipe also called for citric acid, gypsum, non-iodized salt, and yeast food.

"If you're a beginner reading this for the first time," Burch wrote, "you're probably bewildered by now by the mass of unfamiliar terms swarming about your head. Don't panic, though, because explanations are coming up, starting here." He was as good as his word. He wrote clearly and well about plastic fermenters, thermometers, and hydrometers, why and how the last are calibrated. Echoing Nichols, Burch recommended food-grade plastic, not cheap garbage cans or crocks. Along the way, he offered good advice, suggesting the homebrewer should always clean a new primary fermenter with bicarbonate of soda to neutralize any solvents that might be left over from the manufacturing process. He also described the advantages of cheesecloth and secondary fermenters.

In the "Ingredients" section, Burch discussed different kinds of malt (pale malted barley, crystal or caramel malt, black patent malt, Munich malt) and various sugars (dextrose, sucrose, lactose, brown sugar). He devoted three pages to hops, including "flavoring" hops and "aromatic" hops, and explained the difference between leaf hops, hops pellets, and hops extracts. Since Nichols's recipe called for Hallertau hops, I had not looked further, because I was perfectly happy with them at the time, but Burch described hops with evocative names like Pride of Ringwood, Talisman, Brewer's Gold, Cluster, and Northern Brewer. He classified them objectively according to their relative bitterness, and subjectively according to their aroma.

I also learned more about yeast, that marvelous, mysterious, single-celled creature that is the *sine qua non* of baking and brewing. I came to understand the distinction between the top-fermenting strain used for ales and the bottom-fermenting variety common to lagers.

Baker's yeast does work for beer, but it has several major drawbacks, Burch said. It reproduces best at higher temperatures, where the threat of infection is much greater; it doesn't settle well, and thus homebrew made with it is always cloudy. Finally, it was developed to create the maximum amount of carbon dioxide to make bread rise. Now I understand why my early beers tasted so yeasty.

Under "Optional Equipment," Burch listed items like a bottle-washer sprayer that could be attached to a kitchen faucet, hose clamps to aid in bottling, and an office scale for measuring small amounts of hops. Other items were familiar—good, solid, returnable green or dark-brown bottles and a strong capper. I felt like a pioneer, long in the woods, who happens upon a general store.

When I finished the book, I thought ruefully how helpful it would have been five years earlier, when I'd started brewing. But it hadn't been available then. Fortunately, I didn't have to look far to find some of the supplies he wrote about. Garden Way Living Center, a division of the Garden Way companies devoted to self-sufficient living, had several shelves of home wine- and beermaking paraphernalia.

However, for all the richness of its selection, the store did not carry any of the flavoring hops varieties Burch recommended for his light-bodied pale ale. All it offered was Fuggles, Cascades (which Burch recommended for aromatic hops), and my old workhorse, Hallertau. On the spot I formulated a rule of thumb for the homebrewer: Be flexible. Never be afraid to substitute and create your own recipes, because no homebrew store is ever likely to carry all the exact ingredients required for any but the most elementary of recipes.

The major purchase from Garden Way was my first hydrometer. Burch thought it indispensable. As a "brewer's compass," it allows you to measure the progressive conversion of sugars into alcohol and carbon dioxide. The hydrometer calculates the specific gravity or weight of the liquid. Sugar dissolved in water is denser or heavier than plain water, whereas alcohol is lighter. As the yeast converts sugars, the density of the solution falls and thus the hydrometer will sink lower in the solution. The scale inside the instrument shows the potential alcohol when you start, so you can accurately predict what the final alcoholic content will be.

Burch explained that the higher the ratio of malt sugars to corn sugars, the higher the final gravity will be, because malt sugars are not refined enough to convert completely. Some of their solids always remain in solution and keep the final gravity above 1,000. Burch made this explanation clear and concise, but another homebrew book quite blithely ordered the brewer to bottle only when gravity reached zero. Once a friend of mine left a batch in the secondary for three months, waiting for it to reach that impossible figure.

The best ingredients and recipes are only as good as the containers in which the brewing occurs. Cleanliness here is as close to goodness as it is to godliness. Thanks again to Burch, I learned about the marvels of bleach and sodium metabisulphite. Chlorine bleach is an excellent sterilizer and cleanser when used carefully and rinsed out thoroughly. If bleach is followed by a rinse of sodium metabisulphite, the vessels and bottles will have no residual film or aftertaste and should be clean enough to thwart all infection. Conversely, I finally understood that soap and detergents are anathema to good beer, because of the film they leave behind. That is why many bars don't use soap on their beer glasses—soap and detergent kill the head. The head may be extraneous to the taste, but beer without a head looks more like ginger ale than beer.

In the next year, I made six or eight batches from Burch's book: pale ales, brown ales, lagers, and a "steam beer." I experimented with adding small amounts of salt, gypsum, citric acid, and gelatin to clear the beer. I really couldn't tell if these ingredients helped the taste, but they made me feel more professional.

Overall, Burch's beers were noticeably better than my Grand Rapids lager, although the difference between them was not as great as between Grand Rapids and the original Blue Ribbon brew. I loved to experiment with different ratios of malt to hops in the hope I could approximate some of the great beers of the world, like Guinness or Spaten Bräu. That I didn't come close didn't matter.

Homebrew began to find a niche as a liquid "thank you." It became an offering of something more personal than money or words. I have given beer to the town employee who graded our dirt road in St. Johnsbury. I have used it to thank the plumber for fixing our furnace on a wild wintry night. The manager of the restaurant supply store where I buy brewing equipment earned a bottle for his help in finding a stainless steel pot. When we burden the garbage man with extra debris, he gets a homebrew. The stereo repairman who fixed a receiver free of charge won a six-pack of porter.

Exchanging beer for services probably placed me in the underground economy and, thanks to bartering, I made another convert.

Professor Peter Seybolt is a man of many parts—a good tennis player, fly-fisherman, and pig farmer as well as a teacher of Chinese history. In his farming capacity, Peter asked us to trade some of our labor for some of his spiced sausage. I brought a six-pack of homebrew to drink as we ground and packed the slippery meat. Then we invited him to help us bottle a batch in return for more homebrew. As we bottled, he became so intrigued that he went to Garden Way and bought all the necessary equipment.

My reputation as a homebrewer began to spread like the smell of french fries out of a diner's ventilator. This was literally as well as figuratively so, for when I brewed a batch and turned on the exhaust fan above the stove, one could smell the Mares brewery three houses away.

One evening, during a conversation with friends who owned a small construction company, I learned they had registered the name Lake Champlain Monster Brewing Company with the Secretary of State. The name referred to the local version of the much-sought denizen of Loch Ness. That summer there was a flurry of "sightings" of the monster. A minor tourist attraction was born. Although they were not brewers, these friends were hearty beer drinkers who dreamed of a combination saloon and brewery that would dispense Monster Beer to students and tourists. I was intrigued enough by the idea to suggest an intermediate step—put a notice in the paper to solicit interest in a homebrewing club. I thought these future commercial brewers ought to have some practical experience.

The organizational meeting of the Vermont Brewers Association took place at the construction company's warehouse one warm August evening. Each person was to bring a six-pack or its equivalent of his favorite beer. I was the only one to bring homebrew. The others provided the likes of Fischer's, Guinness, Beck's, and Moosehead.

I knew all seven people present except Barton Merle-Smith, late of Boulder, Colorado, and then the owner of Barton's Hot Tubs in Burlington. Barton's ample midsection was covered by a stained T-shirt emblazoned with an emblem of the American Homebrewers Association: a smiling turkey clasping sheaves of barley in one foot and an overflowing bottle of homebrew in the other.

It was soon apparent that Barton knew a lot more about homebrew than I did. For an hour he regaled us with stories about brewing in Boulder and the American Homebrewers Association. The AHA, we learned, had been founded early in the 1970s by a nuclear-engineering dropout and alternative-school teacher named Charlie Papazian. He began teaching homebrewing for a little extra cash and launched the organization out of a spare room in his house. He applied for and received tax-exempt status from the Internal Revenue Service, which made contributions tax-deductible. Here was a philanthropic organization dedicated to spreading the gospel of homebrew. Barton passed around copies of the AHA journal, *Zymurgy,* the only magazine I've ever seen that defines its title on the cover. "Zymurgy: dealing with the fermentation process, as in brewing." The motto of the AHA is "Relax. Don't Worry. Have a Homebrew!" When I later sent them $50, I became a Diamond-Studded Platinum Mug Sponsor with a membership card which expired "Never."

Barton's first brew was called Long Distance Lager, because he had made it according to directions from his brother in Boulder during a two-hour telephone call. Like a film dissolve, that story merged into his description of a "beer and steer," where a whole cow was roasted and the guests consumed five or ten kegs of homebrew and then jumped naked into a bank of hot tubs.

Zymurgy was full of good information, book reviews, discussions of technique, and accounts of local and national homebrewing contests. There were recipes with names like Danger Knows No Favorites Dark Lager, Goat Scrotum Ale, and Whitey's No-Show Ale. Sprinkled throughout its well-illustrated pages were anecdotes and one-liners. Stealing from Fat Freddy of the Fabulous Furry Freak Brothers comics, one wag paraphrased, "Homebrew will get you through times of no money better than money will get you through times of no homebrew."

P. T. Davis of Seattle captured the spirit of homebrewing when he wrote in the Letters column: "I survived Mt. St. Helens, although not by much—drank too much homebrew Saturday night, May 17, and overslept, thus did not arrive at Spirit Lake in time for my demise. Relax and have a homebrew. It saves lives from volcanoes and no doubt from other disasters as well."

Even the club notes brought chuckles for some of the names. Besides the Maltose Falcons and San Andreas Malts, there were the Mile-high Masterspargers, Redwood Lagers, San Gabriel Valley Wort Hogs, and the Christian Ferment League at Princeton Theological Seminary in New Jersey.

Zymurgy was the real revelation of that first Vermont Brewers Association meeting. It introduced me to a whole subculture of homebrewers. These were not people who just poured more sugar into the brew to give it a bigger alcohol boost. Nor were they old-line, stalwart homebrewers who were satisfied with Blue Ribbon malt. Brewing was part of their lives, just like buying coffee or planting peas in the spring. They formed a collection of serious beermaking cranks, technocrats, and mavericks who still valued the fences of good recipes and directions. They were restless experimenters who enjoyed what one called their "mud-pies-for-adults" activity.

The fledgling Association aside, I was feeling again those itches of boredom I had noticed after mastering Grand Rapids lager. I was like the novice sky-diver who tires of static line jumps as he dreams of free-fall. The more I read *Zymurgy* and *Amateur Brewer* (an advanced homebrewing newsletter from Portland, Oregon), the more I was convinced that first-class brewing went far beyond malt extracts and hops pellets.

To reach that special state of grace and accomplishment, I had to enter the world of "all-grain brewing." It required learning techniques I had only read about, like mashing, sparging, and water treatment. For advanced brewers, "all-grain" means grinding the malted barley, mashing it, and straining out the sugars (sparging), all before getting to the point where an extract brewer opens a can of malt syrup or a bag of powdered malt.

Since leaving Grand Rapids and Nichols's store, I had made a habit of visiting homebrewing suppliers wherever I found them. One of those was Winemakers Supplies in Northampton, Massachusetts, owned by Frank Romanowski.

Romanowski had been a baker who, fifteen years earlier, began making his own wine. This led him to stocking and selling home winemaking supplies. In a few years, the winemaking business exceeded that of the bakery. His store was a bit smaller than Nichols's, but it seemed to have both more equipment and a greater variety of ingredients: six kinds of hops, for example. Romanowski and his wife ran the business with the help of George Peppard (not the actor), who had worked for four months at an English brewery and had dreams of opening his own place in nearby Easthampton.

On my second trip to Northampton, Romanowski offered some of his own pale ale. It was superb—smooth, mellow, and as good as any English bitter I had ever drunk. "This is all-grain beer," he said. "No matter how hard you try, you simply cannot duplicate this with extracts, because extracts cannot provide enough body." I *had* to make all-grain beer. Impatient brewer that I am, I didn't bother to question Romanowski about the technique. I assumed the admirable Burch would tell me all about it in his book. I bought twenty pounds of "two-row" barley and declined Romanowski's offer to grind it for an extra 10 cents per pound.

At home, the first task therefore was to grind the barley, but I now realized I had no idea how fine to make it. Five messy minutes with a rolling pin sent me to the coffee grinder. Using its coarsest setting, I finished the job in twenty minutes, and left a fine layer of grain dust on every horizontal surface of the kitchen.

It suddenly dawned on me that this was not going to be easy.

The next mistake I made was mashing at too high a temperature and not getting the right amount of mash. Then another batch boiled over. Gradually, I improved, though I still needed a day to complete all the steps. I added up the pros and cons. Romanowski's all-grain beer

was 75 to 100 percent better than any extract I had ever made, but it also too three times longer. Was it worth it?

Just as I was about to quit again, two things happened. First, Charlie Papazian published his book, *The Joy of Homebrewing*. For me and hundreds of thousands of others, it became the Bible of homebrewing with its exhaustive and approachable details. Then, Tom and Ellen Ayres opened a homebrewing supply store in my town called Something's Brewing. Their ingredients were better than Romanowski's; their techniques and equipment were more advanced, and the shop was only one mile away from my house.

Best of all they introduced me to five-gallon soda kegs, which, with a carbon-dioxide attachment, allowed me to keg my beer and keep it ready in my basement for all occasions. With all those improvements and the reduced time it all took, I reached a comfortable homebrew cruising altitude

∂ 5 ∿

A Busman's Holiday

One fall afternoon, the postman brought the usual load of political appeals, junk mail, three newspapers, and a few pieces of legitimate first-class mail. Almost lost among the flashy catalogues for tools and kitchenware was a brown package from Chris's sister, who was then studying in England. Inside was a paperback book entitled The Good Beer Guide published by the Campaign for Real Ale (CAMRA).

In language reminiscent of a nineteenth-century broadside, the *Guide* began:

> Ladies and Gentlemen of the Drinking Public. Once again the Campaign for Real Ale presents for your delectation almost 6,000 of the very Finest Hostelries in these Islands that dispense that great delight: Traditional Draft Beer. Members of the Campaign have spared no effort to seek out Sundry Inns, Taverns and Public Houses that keep and serve their Ale in the most Excellent of Condition.

"Traditional draft beer or ale," the jacket cover continued, "is brewed only from malted barley, water, hops, and yeast to make the bitters, milds, and porters. The means of dispensing are several—from the cask, the beer engine, or electric power—but all these Systems eschew the Noisome Carbonic Gas which the Purveyors of Inferior Brew use to mask the Lackluster Taste of their Dubious Products."

Here were words to warm the heart of all brewing purists. I spent the evening with a pint of homebrewed porter, perusing the *Guide* as dreamily as a dedicated pub crawler might examine a map of London.

The *Guide* gave a brief history of the venerable English pub, telling how that institution was the outgrowth of hearty private hospitality. It also listed all of the nation's 170 operating breweries along with their addresses and telephone numbers.

Both Chris and I had been to England several times, and she had lived there for seven years—albeit before she reached drinking age. We liked the hearty English ales and stouts. Four years earlier, we had driven around southern Ireland and in twelve days managed to explore some forty-four bars and the bottoms of countless glasses of Guinness, Murphy's, and Smithwick's Ale. We were experienced, if not hardened, pub crawlers.

Why not make a vacation of visiting some of these small breweries listed in the CAMRA *Guide?* I had toured two breweries in this country, the Anheuser-Busch plant in Merrimack, New Hampshire (capacity 3 million barrels a year), and the world's largest brewery, Coors, in Golden, Colorado (15 million barrels). These were not breweries, they were factories—as impersonal and sterile and remote from good beer as giant bakeries are from homemade bread. The CAMRA *Guide* described small breweries producing as little as a hundred gallons per week.

We had friends in Oxfordshire who would find us a place to stay, and a quick look at the *Guide* revealed seven breweries within thirty miles of Stonesfield, our prospective base. We contacted our friends and dispatched letters to those seven breweries, asking if we could tour their establishments. We didn't expect any replies; we only hoped they would be hospitable when we arrived.

Once settled in Stonesfield, a village of three hundred people, surrounded by barley fields, we tried its three pubs. The nearest was a Courage outlet, the Black Sheep, which was longer on boisterous dart-contest atmosphere than on real ale. Then we headed for the two largest breweries on the list, Morrell's in Oxford and Morland's in Abingdon. Morrell's annual production is 40,000 barrels, and Morland's is 70,000. (The English barrel is thirty-six gallons, whereas an American barrel is thirty-one gallons.) Both head brewers had received our letters and gave us personally conducted tours.

By American standards, Morrell's and Morland's are tiny, about one-twentieth the size of an average U.S. brewery, but compared with my ten-gallon basement brewery, they were enormous. Thanks to my homebrewing experience, however, I found it easy and enjoyable to follow the process from grinding through mashing, sparging, boiling, and fermentation to kegging. At the end, the brewers served us some of their products in employees' tap rooms. Both breweries were over a hundred years old, but their equipment was relatively new and thus lacked the architectural romance one associates with an old-fashioned facility.

Tradition greeted us in spades at the Hook Norton Brewery, about thirty miles west of Oxford. Hook Norton is one of the few remaining "tower breweries"—great, classic, five-story wooden structures built in the late nineteenth century. Louvers in the Victorian cupola vented the brew kettles' steam, and on this chill December morning, great clouds wreathed the upper stories.

David Clarke, third-generation brewer and owner, led us through the brewery from top to bottom, just as the grain, hops, and water progress from the tower down to the basement casking operation. "We're dragging ourselves into the nineteenth century," he quipped as he showed us the 1890 steam engine and the 1920s "coppers," or boilers. Only the white plastic fermenting vessels looked contemporary. In the middle of the tour, Clarke paused for five minutes to help an employee add Fuggles and Comet hops and a small amount of dark malt extract to a brew. Then it was down into the basement, where, in a corner, Clarke served us half-pints of his three ales. He drew the beer directly from wooden kegs placed there for the employees. They were all delicious, especially Old Hookey, a well-hopped, darker ale.

We next drove to the rolling Cotswold hills laced with sheep farms and fields of brussels sprouts and barley. In a small valley north of Stow-on-the-Wold, we found a brewery that gave new dimension to the word *idyllic*. In a series of connected stone buildings dating back to the fifteenth century, L. Claude Arkell brews twenty barrels of pale ale daily for his seventeen tied houses and inns. The brewery stands beside a trout pond whose denizens feed on some of the spent grains, while above them float stately black swans, geese, and ducks. Water from the pond turns a mill wheel that is connected to Arkell's grain grinder. Twenty years ago, Arkell harvested his own barley, malted it in one part of the barn, and used the product in his beer. Now he buys the barley locally. Hops come from nearby Worcestershire.

He seemed so devoted to his brewery and so matter-of-fact about its operation that we asked what it would take to start a brewery from scratch and operate it profitably.

"It wouldn't be so hard," Arkell said. "I never went to brewing school. I learned from other brewers, picked their brains, kept my mouth shut. Good brewing is really only four things: get your water chemistry right, watch your brewing temperature, clean the pipes, and use your noddle." He surely made it seem simple and straightforward. What a life—to build a brewery by a trout pond, raise sheep and fruit trees on the hillside, feed the geese and swans at dusk.

Arkell said he spends as much time as he can with other brewers, because he feels he can always learn more. One of them had recently introduced him to some new hops pellets that Arkell now used most of the time.

"You know, the big brewers could crush me in a second," he said. "But they won't, because the influence of CAMRA has made them shy of public censure. I am worried about the growth of homebrewing kits, because they aren't taxed. Taxes are what make beer so expensive in the pub.

"I'm a third-generation brewer. If you want to see someone who started from scratch, visit Tom Litt. He buys yeast from me once a week."

Litt was already on our list, so we headed for the village of South Leigh, home of the Mason Arms. We had been intrigued with CAMRA's description of Litt's pub as a "homebrewery." There, behind the bar, across from a warm oak log fire, we found him engaged in a lively discussion with a customer. They were talking about the Celebration Ale that Litt had brewed to commemorate the marriage of Prince Charles and Lady Diana.

Litt remembered our letter and invited us to come back in the morning. "In the meantime, these are on the house," he said. He handed each of us a pint of Sowlye (South Leigh) Ale, his one and only brew. It was a fine beer, malty yet hopped enough to be memorable.

When we arrived the next morning, we could see the steam rising from a former stable behind the inn. We found Litt stoking an ancient, rusty, coal-fired boiler. As he scampered between the boiler room, brewhouse, and "cellar" (an enclosed horse stall), he told us how he came to brew.

A farmer's son, Litt had bought the run-down farmhouse in 1964, converted it to an inn, and added a restaurant that was good enough to draw people out of Oxford for luncheon. This success made him restless for more challenge, and in 1974, on a half-serious bet, he assembled some equipment and brewed a seventy-five-gallon batch of beer, which, his surprised friends had to agree, was good. Over the next twelve months, he refined both equipment and recipe until he was satisfied. Only one vessel, the hundred-gallon boiling kettle, was built to order. The rest was surplus equipment: a potato cooker from the army, coolers from a dairy, used kegs from other breweries, and a thirty-year-old coal-fired steam boiler. His total investment was less than $10,000.

Tom Litt exuded enthusiasm and pragmatism. He nursed the boiler as if it were human. He used no special water treatment. His conditioning room, where the beer ages in kegs for six to twelve days, was simply an enclosed and cooled horse stall. When the beer was ready to drink, he rolled the keg across the parking lot and tapped it in a room behind his simple bar.

"There's no mystery in brewing. Just keep the place clean. The trouble with most brewers is that they are never satisfied. They are always trying to change this ingredient or that procedure."

"Do you have any problem with health inspectors?" I asked.

48

"None at all. They know that if I don't keep the brewery clean the beer will spoil and people won't buy it." As for the tax collector, the district officer had a key to the stable and he could and did come in at odd hours to check the correlation between the ingredients Litt buys and the amount of beer he sells.

As we watched, Litt climbed a ladder with a five-gallon plastic bucket and emptied its dark syrupy contents into the boiler.

"What's that?" I asked.

"Malt extract."

"Malt extract!" I gasped. "You mean you don't mash?"

"Of course not. Why should I? I can make perfectly good beer with the extracts and save time and trouble and expense."

I reeled at the simplicity of it all. Unless I had a tin tongue, he was making an extract ale fully as good as any mashed version I could produce. What was he doing right, and what was I doing wrong?

As he puttered around the brewery, Litt dictated the recipe for his Sowlye Ale (O.G. 1037):

100 gals. water
100 lbs. Edme liquid
malt extract
3 lbs. Golding hops
3 lbs. liquid yeast from Arkell
1 pint finings at kegging time
handful of loose Goldiongs for finishing hops at the end

Boil for an hour, cool it down using a dairy cooler, pump it into
the primary fermenter for four days, then into kegs for about
ten days, and it's ready to drink.

Was it the wooden kegs he used that made the beer so good? No, they were lined with stainless steel and gave off no special taste. Was it Litt's careful handling? He was no more careful than I was. Was I exaggerating the ambience of South Leigh, Oxfordshire? Perhaps. But that still did not explain it all. How he made such good beer so simply gnawed at me for the rest of our stay in England.

The key to Litt's financial success lay in his reliance on the brewery for only a portion, in his case roughly one-third, of his income. The inn and restaurant provided the other two-thirds. It would be impossible, he said, to make a living from the brewery alone. Nor would he want to. Litt was quite happy to spend only one day a week brewing enough beer to sell in the following week. His seemed a very civilized existence.

Fifty miles away in London, David Bruce was anything but content with a hundred gallons a week. Bruce is the founder of five brewpubs, four in London and one in Bristol. His menagerie of pubs have names like The Fox and Firkin, Goose and Firkin, Frog and Firkin, etc. A former manager at Courage's and Theakston's (a small Yorkshire brewery), Bruce took a third mortgage on his London house to launch the first Firkin and in four years was grossing $4 million annually.

By the time Bruce got to London in 1978, there were only four brewpubs extant in England, one of them in the city. Bruce believed that the public was ready for a new round of brewpubs if done with flair. He bought old, mostly run-down pubs and put breweries in the cellars. One pub featured a porthole, another a glass section in the floor through which customers could watch the beer being brewed. Bruce sold beers with such arresting names as Dogbolter, Earthstopper, and Sphincter Special. He produced T-shirts and buttons and formed clubs of regular drinkers. In short, "We're a marketing organization as much as a production organization," said the chief lieutenant, Andy MacDonald.

When we told him that the visit to South Leigh had aroused our interest in tiny commercial brewing, Bruce told us to drive down to Ringwood and see the brewery there. "They've made beer for us when we've run short. What's more, they are selling whole brewery kits—plans, equipment, and all. They even take on students."

The Ringwood Brewery was located in a couple of unpretentious stucco buildings on a back street. The mash tun and boiler with their wooden insulating jackets looked more like hot tubs than brewing vessels. The kegging operation brought to mind the disarray of a bus company repair shop. Ringwood brews its own beer and distributes it to the free trade (nontied houses) nearby, but its bread and butter has been selling the plans and, when possible, the actual equipment for microbreweries across Great Britain. The cost was roughly $40,000 for plans and equipment for a brewery with a capacity of ten to fifteen barrels. When we visited Ringwood, they had sold about a dozen brewery kits.

Two other factors made the trip to Ringwood worthwhile. It was the first time we had heard of beer sold right out of the brewery. Customers brought their own jugs or purchased them from the brewery and took them home full of porter, bitter, Forty-Niner, or Old Thumper. This retail share of the business had risen to 25 percent in just one year. Ringwood's ales were respectable, but not as good as Hook Norton's or Arkell's.

The second discovery at Ringwood was the name of an American who had served an apprenticeship there. He was William Newman, of Albany, New York, who had fallen in love with English ale and decided to build a brewery in the United States. In 1979, he had worked at Ringwood for four months and then bought the plans for his own operation. The vision of an American single-handedly proposing to blow foam literally and figuratively in the face of the American giants was most intriguing. We would go see him when we returned home.

❧ 6 ❧

"Many Are Called..."

In the first months after we returned from Britain, I read a number of articles about small breweries in the United States. Almost every issue of *Zymurgy* and *Brewers Digest* included reports of "microbreweries" in California or Colorado or Oregon. These new breweries produced from several hundred to over a thousand barrels per year, except for Anchor Brewing Company in San Francisco, which sold about 25,000 barrels of the incomparable Anchor Steam Beer and Anchor Porter. All the microbreweries in the country hardly threatened the giants. With annual production of 59 million barrels, Budweiser made more beer in three hours than did all the microbreweries in a year.

In contrast to the hundreds and thousands of employees at the big breweries, the micros were often one- and two-person operations, founded by former homebrewers who were longer on love and ingenuity than money. Nonetheless, the articles painted pictures of near-universal success. "We're selling all we can make," was a recurrent comment one read in numerous articles.

There's a bit of the host in each of us. I had once dreamed of running a restaurant. This fantasy stemmed from my grandfather's experience in Helena, Montana, a hundred years ago. He and his brother, immigrants from Bohemia, had established a recreational area called Central Park outside Helena, the state capital. By trolley or horse, citizens had ridden out of town to enjoy baseball fields, a bandstand, a small zoo, and a beer garden serving schooners and kegs of lager from the nearby Horsky and Kessler breweries. Now that I was a brewer, my imagination leaped to the same kind of hospitality, only this included pouring tankards of my own ale, lager, and stout.

During the next months, I offered more and more of my beer to friends and strangers. This was low-cost market research, which, in a way, I had performed since my first offerings of Prohibition Pilsner. Those who liked it, I asked: Would you ever pay money for this beer? How much? What kind of container would you like to see? How important is the label or what the advertising says? Those (blissfully) few who admitted to not liking the beer, I asked how it might be improved.

And the public. Wouldn't it respond enthusiastically to a beer made in Vermont, with its image of purity, hard work, and virtue? Wouldn't the tourists and out-of-state students who flocked the hills and slopes for hiking and skiing, also crowd the bars to drink fine hand-crafted Vermont brews? If I made an intriguing enough label, wouldn't they then take the bottles home to Boston or New York as collectors' items?

About this time, my brother sent me an article from the packaging-industry trade journal *Beverage World*. Under the title "The Bell Doesn't Toll for All Small Breweries," Harold O. Davidson voiced unexpected optimism about the future of small breweries. In contrast to the general expectation of further concentration within the industry, Davidson pointed to a limit on economies of scale. Beyond a certain figure, it would become too expensive to transport a product of 96 percent water. This limitation provided an opening for small and regional breweries. Citing a study by the Stanford Research Institute, Davidson foresaw a "micro-segmentation" within the industry. The market, he forecast, would split into specialized sectors and progressively subdivide as an increased percentage of the population followed more individualistic buying patterns. In other words, more people were becoming open to more flavorful beers, and they were ready to vote their palates and not be led by mass advertising gimmicks. I was encouraged to believe that such microbreweries might have a chance, depending upon how and where they marketed their products.

Enough dreaming. Albany, New York, was only four hours away, and home to the William S. Newman Brewing Company. It was time to visit one of these fledgling breweries.

In a weedy, seedy industrial area a mile from downtown Albany, Chris and I found Newman's brewery. Only a bright new green-and-white sign announcing BREWERY distinguished the building from half a dozen other run-down brick warehouses nearby. The structure had been a mattress factory until fire gutted its innards, leaving it abandoned for thirty years. William Newman was a tall, lean, intense man in tie, sweater, heavy trousers, and rubber boots. A former newspaper editor, teacher, laborer, and state budget analyst, Newman explained that his inspiration arose from an English vacation when he called on small breweries.

After visits to several small American breweries, like D. G. Yuengling & Sons in Pottsville, Pennsylvania, and Anchor Brewing Company in San Francisco, Newman went back to England for a four-month Ringwood apprenticeship. Upon his return to Albany, he spent half a year assembling his construction and financing package. His biggest problem was not raising the money ($250,000 of bank financing, city and state development loans, and his own savings) or formulating a brew, but finding a suitable location. His first choice, in a light industrial zone, adjoined a Fundamentalist church. Unhappy at the prospect of a brewery next door, the congregation successfully opposed his permit application. Newman turned to the abandoned mattress factory.

As I entered the building, I was greeted by a jerry-rigged bar in one corner and the entrance to a small office in another. Copying Ringwood's practice, Newman sold beer straight from the keg in returnable plastic containers. He said this method already accounted for a third of his sales. From there we passed into his newly painted and insulated "brewhouse," which contained the boiling vessel, hops separator, and four thousand-gallon fermenters. The largest room in the 10,000-square-foot building served a mixture of purposes: grain storage and grinding, a six-hundred-gallon mash tun, and keg washing and filling. Newman had decided to keg his entire production. "It's cheaper and simpler," he said. "I'm surprised that other small breweries are bottling. When you bottle, you have to buy all the containers. You need bottle soakers, fillers, crowners, labelers. And the time involved! Small-scale bottling equipment is hard to find. And then how do you maintain it?"

Total production time, from grinding grain to tapping a keg at a bar, was two and a half weeks. Newman's Pale Ale used Ringwood's recipe and yeast. The barley was American, while the hops were a mixture of American, British, and German varieties.

Newman said that the Albany area had a higher-than-average draft beer consumption rate, and he hoped this would help make his beer the local favorite. Since his beer tasted best around 50°F., he insisted that the bars serve it at that temperature, or else buy a specially built cooler that could do the job. Furthermore, he required that they wait at least twelve hours before serving the beer, so that the yeast could settle. (It seemed to me that these strictures might reduce sales, but I didn't say anything.)

From the brewery, we went next door to the Thatcher Street Pub, a working class bar and one of Newman's best customers. We ordered hamburgers while Newman fetched a fistful of steins and sat down opposite us. As we raised glasses, my mind suddenly went back to the first time I had offered my beer to friends. Bill Newman had the same look on his face. Suppose the beer was terrible. What should I say? I began dredging my vocabulary for words of comfort and praise.

I took a sip. Whew! I brightened. It tasted like . . . Ringwood's Forty-Niner. "Tasty," I said diplomatically. Newman relaxed. It was certainly akin to the other traditional ales we had drunk in England. I liked it, but I wondered how it would sell in American Lagerland. How long would it take for Albany palates to adjust to the taste, slight cloudiness, and warmer temperature of Newman's Pale Ale? Newman obviously hoped it would be before his money ran out. There was a precedent—yogurt had caught on in the land of cottage cheese.

My next step was to call the executive secretary of the Brewers Association of America, the trade association for smaller breweries. William O'Shea, a lawyer and brewery advocate by profession, had run the association for over forty years. Nicknamed "Mr. Small Brewery," he also had the sobriquet of "the industry's undertaker" because he had watched the demise of hundreds of American breweries over the four decades. Surely, I thought, he would be sympathetic to questions about starting a small brewery.

If he was, he expressed it in an odd way. After I outlined my dream, he said bluntly, "You're crazy. People come in here or call every week with the idea they are going to build a small brewery, and they don't have a clue about how tough the market is, or what's required to be success-ful." He dismissed most of the microbrewers, or "boutique brewers," as hobbyists who would do little to help the industry. He did concede that one of these new brewers, Jack McAuliffe of the New Albion Brewery in California, had "the right attitude and the necessary mechanical skills to succeed. He built all his own equipment."

"What about Fritz Maytag of Anchor Brewing?" I asked.

"Oh, he's a special case. He knew what he was doing from the beginning."

No one likes to be called a fool, and I smarted from his criticism; if he was an industry spokesman, the industry was hurting. But later, after talking to several small brewers, I realized this judgment was unfair. O'Shea, it turned out, had been a determined and resourceful defender of local and regional brewers. His bluntness bespoke a deep understanding of the difficulties involved and the battle scars from his decades-long rearguard action.

O'Shea gave me one thing besides a chill shower: he confirmed that Maytag and McAuliffe were two of the founding fathers of the micro-brewing movement. Anchor Steam was a world-class beer, as distinctive as Guinness or Pilsner Urquell. About New Albion I knew zero. There was nothing for it but to visit these pioneers. So I headed to California on my own personal Gold Rush.

The Anchor Brewing Company is housed in a cream-colored former coffee factory in a mixed light industrial and residential neighborhood of San Francisco. You climb a flight of stairs to the office and find your-self looking directly onto the brewing floor. Across from the two office desks, through a glass partition, gleam the cones and chimneys of three copper vessels. Through another glass wall is the taproom, whose walls are festooned with old brewing advertising signs, photographs of steam beer breweries, and glass cases of brewing instruments and utensils. A carved oak bar serves beer to visitors and coffee or tea to employees.

One whole corner is devoted to souvenirs, such as belt buckles, T-shirts, aprons, and visors, all bearing the attractive red, blue, green, tan, and white emblem of "Anchor Steam Beer—Made in San Francisco since 1896."

I was shown into a room where a man was on his hands and knees, as intent as a child shooting marbles. He was flipping a two-inch-thick stack of three-by-four-foot sheets of bottle labels. In his well-tailored clothes, he looked more like a Boston investment banker than a brewer. But behind the rimless hexagonal glasses, his eyes were restless, quizzical, and determined. Speaking almost to himself, he said he must decide in twenty-four hours whether the printer should proceed with these eight million labels, which was a year's supply. "Do you realize how many eight million bottles are?" he asked. He was thinking out loud. The blue in the label still did not quite match the blue in the bottle cap: "The color is drifting too much." He wanted them just right. He gave word to have the printer try one more match.

"Now, what can I do for you?" Fritz Maytag asked.

I said I was one more homebrewing moth drawn to the light of commercial brewing and I had come to learn how he'd made Anchor such a successful company.

We sat down at a table where I could look out onto the copper brewing kettles and he told me his story.

In 1965, Fritz Maytag, heir to the washing machine fortune, with a degree in Asian studies from Stanford, was, as he put it, "drifting." He had helped start a dairy business and winery in Chile, and he didn't want to go back to the family trade in Iowa. During a visit to San Francisco, he went to dinner at one of his college haunts, the Spaghetti Factory, where as a student he had drunk schooners of Anchor Steam Beer, a local brew and the last of a great tradition of steam beers.

Steam beer is to beer what the banjo is to musical instruments—America's only genuine contribution to the field. The name is derived from the strong carbonation in the beer when it ferments. It is a hybrid beverage first brewed during the Gold Rush days in the mid-nineteenth century, using lager yeast but at warmer ale-fermenting temperatures. The brewers also included the German-Bohemian system of *kraeusen*-ing—adding some young beer to the aging beer to give it natural carbonation. When kegs of steam beer were tapped, they hissed and foamed in a manner unlike English-style ales. Spectators to the tapping applied the misnomer *steam* to the beer. California then had little or no ice or deep cellars in which to keep the beer cool. At one time, there had been twenty-seven steam beer breweries in San Francisco. By Prohibition, this number had fallen to seven, and by 1965 there was only Anchor, producing fewer than five hundred barrels a year.

At the Spaghetti Factory, Maytag heard that Anchor was for sale. The next day, he visited the brewery and, on an impulse, bought it lock, stock, and lauter tun.

"It was a crazy thing to do. The brewery was a disaster. The equipment was ghastly. The quality was inconsistent. When it was good, it was very good. At its worst, it was pretty bad. Some of the bad beer was getting into the trade and making a poor sales situation worse. They made a batch about every two months. They didn't even boil the wort; they just sort of simmered it. They sold only draft, and the kegs were dirty and leaked."

At first, Maytag simply paid the bills and tried to halt the sales decline. But then he decided he either had to get out or get into the business all the way and make a going concern of it. "I was determined to see this brewery succeed as a real business. I wanted to sell beer at a reasonable price. I wanted to make a real beer, not a gimmick or a joke or a hype.

"I can't say that I bought the brewery with a lot of philosophical intent. It's true that from the first I was infatuated with the mystery of brewing, its alchemical aspects. There is something magical in our culture about the idea of alcohol and mind-altering substances that is moderately accepted. It is a dreadful thing in many ways. A lot of people have been killed by alcohol. Scary stuff. But I think it does a lot more good than harm. Beer is the common man's alcohol. Breweries are places where you literally create beer out of grain—it's really alchemy—turning grain into bubbly, sparkling, magic stuff that affects your attitude— makes you sing songs . . . and cry.

"Setting out to make a high-quality product was my theme from the beginning. I wanted a sense of security about the product because of the way it was made, the methods, equipment, etc. I wanted an old-fashioned, interesting, unusual way of brewing, a story I could talk about. I took what little we had at the brewery and what I could learn about this funny West Coast tradition of steam beer and cast a Platonic ideal of what Anchor Steam Beer would be like if you had all the technology to make it simple and pure."

But to make it pure wasn't so simple. "It took years of building and testing, lots of money on rent and salaries to develop the beer and then sell it as a great local product."

Maytag took a number of brewing courses, but for the most part he taught himself on the job and through reading. He worked on the equipment. He made sure of what was needed and then spent the money to get it—stainless steel and copper everywhere. He received help from people in the dairy industry who had long experience with sanitation.

"We're doing something very weird, which is making beer at warm temperatures—fifties and sixties—and holding it for a month. Sanitation must be our main concern. No brewery can be dirty and make good beer. There are very few organisms which grow in beer, but, boy, do they grow! The way we are doing it, we're asking for trouble—it's like leaving the apple pie to cool on the back porch for a week."

The vessels in which primary fermentation occurs are unique to brewing, being twenty-by-thirty-foot stainless-steel open pans, two and a half feet deep at one end and three and a half feet deep at the other.

It took Maytag five years to build up his sales from 500 to 1,200 barrels annually. In another three years, he reached 7,000 and the company moved into the black for the first time. He began distributing in the Western states, Minnesota, and New Jersey. Anchor was becoming a cult beer. He added an Anchor Porter and pushed the old brewery to its limit of 12,000 barrels.

In 1977, Maytag bought a used German brewhouse with a capacity of 40,000 barrels. He had it shipped to a new, larger building in San Francisco. In a couple of years, he was producing 18,000 barrels to break even, and by 1982 Anchor was distributing 28,500 barrels of steam and porter to twenty states. This is still less than one-thousandth of Budweiser's annual production, but, then, Maytag is assuredly not competing with Budweiser. Anchor is a strong, all-malt brew with four times the hops of the average American beer.

When I told him of my brewery fantasy, Maytag laughed and said scores of people had come to see him with the same dream.

"I try to talk to them all. I tell them that first it takes a lot of money. Industry estimates are a hundred to two hundred dollars per barrel of capacity installed. I think you have to look on the high side of that figure. I could never have done this without inherited money, because no one would lend me the funds. I don't care how charming I was or how good the beer tasted. This is a risky business. The whole country, the whole world, is full of empty breweries.

"Secondly, you need at least one person who will devote unbelievable effort to making good beer. Even so, it takes a lot of luck and a lot of talent, because you can't make a good reputation quickly for a product unless you're very lucky.

"When I took over this brewery, there were only a few imports here, mainly Dos Equis, Guinness, and Heineken. The wine and cheese renaissances hadn't yet taken place, the greening of America was still to come, the whole 'good life' movement hadn't occurred. Americans didn't know yet that they were going to start to enjoy food and drink and savor quality and natural things.

"Beer is just beer. That's part of the problem and part of the fun of it. Wine is anything you want to make of it, but beer is beer. That's one reason I like making beer. On the one hand, it's the common man's drink. Nobody will pay a dollar a bottle for any great quantity of it. On the other hand, it's much harder to make than wine, takes more art and science. The biggest difference from wine is that beer lacks what I call the participation and risks of nature. Classic wine is made from grapes in one location. In good years they're great and in bad years they're bad. When you drink that wine, you participate in that risk.

"To build a successful brewery, you needn't spend as much money as I did, but you do have to sell your product, and that's something homebrewers don't realize. We put in a lot of hours, years, selling here and then moving to Wyoming, Arizona, Boston, and Florida. In the whole Bay Area, we sell maybe two thousand barrels. The reason we range so far is that we can't sell enough here. The beer doesn't sell itself."

Maytag did not spend a lot of money on advertising, certainly nothing to compete with the majors. Instead, he assiduously cultivated opinion makers, newspaper writers, and the public through guided brewery tours. He made sure Anchor was entered in beer tastings around California. Anchor's reputation spread, as beer lovers learned about the funny little dark "steam" beer that held its own against the more heavily advertised European imports.

Probably the most important lesson Maytag learned from all his reading and experimentation was to have near-operating-room cleanliness in his brewhouse. The average visitor looks at the shining brew kettles through the window of the hospitality room, then turns to drink some beer. The alert homebrewer will notice the fanatical maintenance. Maytag went first-class on his equipment, not because he wanted to impress people but because of the need for sanitation.

"Homebrewers don't have this kind of problem. They brew maybe once a week, then put their equipment away until the next batch. If you take a shower once a week, you can have a pretty decrepit shower stall, even a wooden one with a canvas floor. After using it on Saturday night, it will be dry by Monday. Mold won't grow and rot it. But take three showers a day every day, and that shower will practically walk away after a year. In a commercial brewery everything is wet, and unless you clean well every day, you pick up mold and bacteria and wild yeast."

About sixty miles from Maytag's splendid brewery, down a dusty Sonoma road lined with vineyards, I found the New Albion Brewing Company, occupying half of a twenty-by-forty gray metal warehouse. Only a small hand-lettered sign wired to a piece of rusting farm machinery hinted this was a pioneer brewery.

The office was a stark contrast to that of Anchor Brewing. In one corner of the ten-foot-square space was an enormous open safe, inside of which were a pile of brewing texts. Another corner contained advertising and promotional materials, T-shirts, placards, and tabletop displays. The rest of the room was taken up by a large desk covered by books, papers, and two sleeping cats.

Jack McAuliffe had discovered British ales while stationed at an American submarine base in northern Scotland in the 1960s. When he had run short of money to spend at pubs, he found a homebrew supply shop nearby and began making his own beer. By the time he left the navy, McAuliffe had decided to build his own small brewery.

Through eight or nine jobs, including one as an optical engineer in Silicon Valley, McAuliffe nurtured his dream. He chose the name New Albion for his beers because that was the name Sir Francis Drake gave to the San Francisco Bay area when he stopped there on his global circumnavigation in 1579. Drake's ship, the *Golden Hind,* continued its voyage on the New Albion labels.

McAuliffe was as different from Maytag as a bulldog from a greyhound. Whereas Maytag was almost professorial in dress and demeanor, McAuliffe was blue-collar through and through. Whereas Maytag chose his words carefully, McAuliffe spat them out brusquely. Whereas Maytag assembled an immaculate four-story brewery in San Francisco, McAuliffe's reflected his shade-tree mechanical skills. He had built the brewery from government surplus fifty-five-gallon stainless-steel drums.

Every piece of equipment, except for a surplus bottle washer (which he bought for $150), he fabricated himself, including a malt hopper, all the fermentation tanks, and the boiler. The grinding mill he built from scratch, using a design from an 1852 brewing text. He trucked in his brewing water every two weeks from a "secret" spring in the hills above Sonoma. With that water he brewed between five and ten barrels a week, or about 350 barrels per year.

"How did you begin?" I asked him.

"You're a homebrewer," he said. "You know how it is when you and your buddies suck down a couple of your beers and say, 'Jesus, wouldn't it be wonderful to do this for a living?' I like beer. I like making beer. Where else could I pick the labels, the bottles, and the name, choose the recipes, decide who will work for me and who will interview me? Where else could I have kittens on the desk? A brewery is the natural consequence of making your own beer. Now, I've always liked the flow of water, ever since I played in creeks as a kid. And I'm mechanical by nature. Unless you're wealthy beyond the dreams of avarice, you must have mechanical ability. And even if you have all the money you need, you still need that understanding of the process. I like to say that farmers make wine and engineers make beer. You must know water and pumps and numbers. And sanitation is *numero uno*.

"Many people think there's an unlimited demand for this product. Wrong. We make a specialty beer, strongly flavored, more beery than most. To sell that kind of beer in a bar, you have to have one which is not just good, it must be great and elbow the other guys aside. It's a mighty competitive business, and successful brewers play hardball. To run a microbrewery, you need the technical skills to get it out the door. Then you need all the financial knowledge and business skills of running any small business, because brewing is first and foremost a business."

As an example of microbrewery frustrations, McAuliffe explained that he'd originally gone through the traditional distribution system. "However, our beer didn't have the shelf life or the volume of the larger brands. Distributors are the same as in any business—they have no interest in any product *per se*. The only thing they are interested in is how much money they are making. So, if you have a product that's delicate, different, high class, and low volume, you get pushed over into the corner under the fluorescent bulb. And then, when someone on the route wants it, they look around and bring out some which has been sitting there under the worst possible conditions. So we just cut the Gordian knot and went directly to our local retail customers. Want a beer?"

Without waiting for an answer, he fetched two glasses and drew them full from a tap fitted into the wall between his bottling and fermentation rooms. It was mellow, a bit cloudy, and stronger than Newman's Pale Ale. It combined the colder temperature and carbonation expected in America with the full body and aroma of genuine English ale.

After I complimented him on the beer, I asked about the future of microbreweries in this country.

"First there is the image, the romance, the dream. Then there is the reality. As the industry continues to shrink, the products have tended to taste more and more like one another. In this country there is a choice of brands but no choice of style. The larger breweries are brewing for the mass market; they can't afford to make specialty beers.

"However, people are becoming more interested in food that tastes different, and that broadened taste will support more specialty beers. The microbreweries can fill that niche. But they need help in getting their beers onto market shelves."

I told him of all the homebrewers I knew who were fascinated with building and running their own breweries, myself included. McAuliffe gave me a long ironic look and said, "Many are called, that's for sure. How many are *chosen* is yet to be seen."

I left New Albion with a couple of T-shirts, a bottle of beer, and a knapsack of admiration for him. Jack McAuliffe was the sandlot brewer who had turned pro. We homebrewers could admire Maytag's systematic, conscientious resurrection of the moribund Anchor brewery, and we envied the financial resources which allowed him to buy the best equipment. But it was easier to identify with the perseverance, ingenuity, and outright brass of Jack McAuliffe, the solitary, dedicated junk rat and entrepreneur who designed and built his brewery from scratch.

Still, the mote in my mind's eye was whether he could survive. Despite tens of thousands of dollars of free publicity, early entry into the market, and, from all I had heard and could judge, an excellent if sometimes inconsistent product, McAuliffe had never produced more than 350 barrels of beer a year. It was something to ponder.

I had one more stop in California—Bill Owens, the founder of Buffalo Bill's Brewpub. Owens, a former photographer and home-brewer, had built the second brewpub in the U.S. and he was an inde-fatigable champion of this type of brewery. He had even trademarked the name "brewpub." Owens argued that beer was going through the same kind of taste revolution which had occurred in coffee, pasta, and bread. People were searching for more sophisticated flavors *and* they wanted to drink that beer in places where they didn't have to compete with drunks, sports nuts, or truck drivers. What Owens offered was fresh, unfiltered, unpasteurized beer which had only traveled sixty-two feet from the conditioning tank to the bar tap. Customers could watch Owens or his assistant brewer making batches through a glass wall. (He stirred his mash tun with a canoe paddle.) Owens stressed the ambience of the place: no smoking, but some darts, music, and good solid food.

To raise the money for the initial brewpub, Owens sold shares for $2,500 apiece. Despite his marketing skill and a raft of media attention, the shares "did not sell like hotcakes. It took 1,000 phone calls and over a year to sell twenty-seven units" and launch the operation.

Owens was in the middle of raising money for his second brewpub, this one closer to the Bay Area. He had dreams of developing a string of these brewpubs along the entire California coast, much "like the early Spanish missions," he joked. (For a couple of days, I even toyed with the idea of buying a share in the second Buffalo Bill Brewpub. It would certainly be cheaper than doing my own. However, when I called Bill to inquire, he told me that, alas, investors had to be California residents.) Meanwhile, several other brewpubs were under development.

The capital investment for a brewpub was certainly less than for a regular brewery. The profit on a barrel of beer was, Owens contended, four, five, or even six times that of bottled beer.

Of course, by definition, a brewpub included a restaurant, with all its attendant specialized demands and quirks. And the question I needed to have answered was: which was more important—the restaurant or the brewery? In a brewery, you could be an introvert and just brew beer, but in a brewpub you had to be an extrovert and make sure the customers were happy.

Owens had never been to England, never visited Tom Litt or David Bruce, the English brewpublicans. He had created his own distinctive American style of brewpub.

Next stop: New York City.

"Why would a successful thirty-one-year-old executive with a major corporation risk his life savings on a project that almost guarantees he will never be rich?" asked the press release. Because, the ad said rhetorically, Matthew P. Reich had a mission to "bring a distinctive, flavorful, American beer to the American market."

I met Reich in a pinched little office on the lower West Side where he was overseeing the delivery of his beer to delis in Manhattan. At first, Reich had believed his own public relations and assumed it would be easy to raise the $1 million he needed to build his brewery. When he found he could raise no more than a quarter of that, one of his potential investors suggested that he subcontract the beermaking at an existing brewery. Reich was intrigued. "I had seen the kinds of bacterial infection other microbrewers were having. By having a large brewery produce my beer, I would be free to concentrate on marketing. Once you have a good product, the key is marketing. Word of mouth is not enough by itself. A reputation has to be cultured, the way Maytag did it. You have to send your beer to the right people, get the right personalities to write about it."

Reich convinced brewing consultant Joseph Owades to help him formulate New Amsterdam Amber Beer, an all-malt lager with 80 percent pale and 20 percent crystal malt and fresh Cascade and Haller-tau hops. It would ferment at the relatively high temperature of 65° F. The two went to F. X. Matt, president of the West End Brewing Co. in Utica, New York. Matt liked the idea, and, having excess brewing capacity, he agreed to begin producing five-hundred-barrel batches of New Amsterdam.

Reich's market research told him to aim for two male cohorts, the eighteen-to-twenty-four-year-old college crowd and the twenty-four-to-forty-year-old young professionals who drank imported beer for status and flavor. He sold his "connoisseur's beer" in single bottles, in delicatessens and saloons where the customers would be "insensitive" to price. Reich said he expected to be selling eight thousand barrels in three years, by which time he would have raised the money to build his own brewery.

The notion of contracting the beer made great sense—commission an established brewery to make the beer to your specifications. That brewery would know sanitation thoroughly. Then, if the beer didn't sell, the investors, including Reich, would lose only the year's cash flow, not the much larger sum needed for plant and equipment.

After my tour of Newman, Anchor, New Albion, Buffalo Bill's, and New Amsterdam, I remained enthusiastic but was more respectful of the difficulties in becoming a small-time brewer. All recognized the importance of marketing and the complexities of a small business. I admired them for different reasons: Maytag because his beer was the best; McAuliffe because he had built his brewery out of little but sweat and mechanical skill; Newman because he had so much faith in the English-style ales to which I was partial; Owens because of his irrepressible advocacy of brewpubs; and Reich because he opened my eyes to the possibilities of contract brewing. All five American brewers had added the yeast of their experience to the wort of my fantasies. After this concoction fermented, it would be time to subject it to more severe analysis.

❧ 7 ❧

A Savage Commitment

For several months, the dream of my own brewery grew like a benign tapeworm. The last Vermont brewery, Petersen's in Burlington, had closed its taps in 1894. Ninety-plus years was long enough for a beer drought. What's more, with Vermont's established reputation for good cheese, maple syrup, ice cream, and craftsmanship of all kinds, the state begged to have a small brewery offering real ale or lager. Not only would the residents love the beer, but the sixty million people living within a day's drive would surely thirst for a Green Mountain brew. Once I had the tourists hooked, they would do my marketing, carrying the message (and the demand) home to Massachusetts, Connecticut, New York, and beyond.

Everyone I spoke with thought the idea was terrific. But talk was cheap and I knew I couldn't do this alone. I needed to find other people as committed as I, people with serious purpose and . . . deep pockets. Therefore, I invited a selection of friends over one evening to explore the idea of building a small brewery. They were all people who liked my beer or who were homebrewers themselves. They included a lawyer, an investment advisor, an engineering student, a contractor, a community organizer, Barton Merle-Smith, the hot tubs entrepreneur, and Jim Hinkel, the former manager of a whey-processing plant and now a food-equipment broker.

For an hour the conversation ranged across possible names for the brewery, the types of beer we could make, possible locations, vague cost estimates, and customer profiles. I extolled Anchor, New Albion, and Reich's rental-brewery scheme. I told them of the micro-segmentation of the market and the growth of imported beer sales, as well as the homebrewing revolution. The more homebrew we drank, the more the idea glittered. But during a pause in the jollity, Jim raised his hand. He said he had scribbled some notes just before the meeting and he wanted to share them.

"First, I think you need to define the reasons for this venture. Is it to be a hobby or a business? Will it stand alone, or be part of something else, such as a restaurant or pub?

"Second, you must lay out the financial factors in *pro formas* for at least three years. When do you expect to make a profit? How do you plan to raise the money? Have you *talked* to any banks?

"Third, there are marketing questions. Where will your beer fit into the present market? What share do you expect to get in Vermont, in New England, in three years, in five years, in ten years? Who are your competitors? Are you challenging Budweiser, or Genesee, or Heineken? What is your sales plan? You need at least a three-year unit-pricing forecast. What promotional programs do you have in mind?"

I gulped and looked around the room. The others were squirming, too, but Hinkel wasn't finished.

"Fourth, there are construction factors. What are the state and federal regulations on building a brewery? You'll need state and federal licenses, local zoning and building permits, affordable space! Will you need a special permit for dumping waste water? Have you considered the taxes on a brewery? What size brewery will you build? Can you find equipment off the shelf, or must it all be custom-made? What is your construction budget? Remember, whatever you calculate, expect it to double.

"Fifth, what are your personnel requirements? If you spend all your time brewing, who will manage the operation? How will you train your help? What will you pay them? And how will you distribute this wonderful beer of yours?"

Hinkel paused to catch his breath. "Those are just a few notes. I haven't even touched on financing, distributors, suppliers, utilities, et cetera, et cetera."

The et ceteras tolled like a clock on Death Row. Jim Hinkel wasn't telling me to go back to the drawing board; in his opinion, I hadn't even entered the drafting room.

After recovering from Hinkel's reality check, it was also obvious that far more serious study was called for. I began plowing through some brewing textbooks, with the sinking feeling I would have to learn a lot of microbiology, business and marketing. I talked to as many micro-brewers as I could find. When the American Homebrewers Association expanded its annual convention to include micro-brewing workshops, I joined scores of people in Boulder for lectures on malt, equipping a brewery, mashing theory, packaging, beer styles, and hops utilization. The group ranged across the spectrum from glassy-eyed hippies from out of the mountains to a Virginia veterinarian who brewed so frequently that he had refrigerated an entire room for storage and was now trying to raise $300,000 for the giant step into commercial brewing. David Bruce flew in from London to talk about his brewpubs. I went home with a candle, if not a fire, rekindled in my belly. I started looking for short courses in brewing science, microbiology, and something about financial projections and packaging.

But then I took a detour from my brewing career—onto the road of politics. I won election to the Vermont House of Representatives. Even though the office was a part-time duty, there was no way I could do much about a brewery while in the legislature. Also, by then we had two small children. Re-election further postponed my commercial brewing career.

While I wrestled with the issues of income taxes, welfare reform, banking regulation, school financing, and minimum sentencing, others were building breweries all across the country. Several of the people I had met in Boulder were among them. In California, breweries sprang up like Topsy. Portland, Oregon, was another hotbed of microbrewing. In Helena, Montana, several entrepreneurs bought the Kessler name and launched a new Kessler beer. Here in Vermont, Steve Mason, a former physical education instructor, and homebrewer, Alan Davis, launched Catamount Brewing Company. Steve had brought some sample brews and his plans to our homebrew club. The beer was well balanced, hoppy, and flavorful. But Jim Hinkel had just singed our ears with skepticism, so we passed those sentiments on to Steve. He and Alan were undaunted, and their brewery opened its spigots. When I bought my first six-pack at the local market, my envy was washed away in the delight of drinking well-crafted specialty beers made in our own backyard. A brewing revolution was under way.

Such enthusiasm over brewery births was tempered by the obituaries. Charles Coury of the Cartwright Brewing Company in Portland believed that his seventeen years of winemaking would make brewing "as easy as falling off a log." "I was a little arrogant," he said. "The differences in degree were so great they became differences in kind. I wish I could have labeled the beer Brew Number One, Number Two, et cetera, and then on the back of the label asked for comments. Everyone expected the first beer to be perfect. In retrospect, it takes quite a bit of wasted beer to break in the equipment and get the right taste." After a year and a half and $100,000, he closed.

Fred Eckhardt, an Oregon beer guru who had acted as an informal adviser to Coury, commented, "The things he wanted to do, he didn't have the equipment for. The things he should have done he didn't recognize the need for. So he went more than a year trying to solve technical problems and competing with people he shouldn't have competed with. His market was people with a taste that says, 'Love me or hate me.' He finally got around to changing the formula, and it was pretty good. But by then it was too late."

Matthew Reich went ahead and built a brewery in New York City, where he brewed for two years, but finally sold the label to his former contractor, F. X. Matt. Reich, who has since moved on to organizing international bicycle races, said he was defeated by the costs of brewing in Manhattan. He could make an operating profit, but, as he told *American Brewer* in the spring of 1992: "... a return on investment? No. It's just that the overhead in New York is different from that in Norwalk,

Connecticut. It's a different animal."

William Newman found, to his woe, that his style of beer and distribution system were out of step with American drinking habits. Also failing to find the money for a bottling line, Newman was forced to lease his brewing equipment to another brewery and to begin contracting for his own beers.

There were other failures. River City Brewing Company in Sacramento and the first Boulder Brewing Company both were overwhelmed by the relentless forces of the market.

"We found that making beer, despite its many difficulties, was the easy part, maybe fifteen percent of the business," said one of Boulder's founders. "Forget the romance of experimenting with different kinds of hops and malts. You've got more important things to think about, like keeping the beer free of bacteria and then selling what you make."

Saddest of all was the demise of New Albion. Jack McAuliffe was never able to get his production and consistency up to profit-making levels, and he couldn't raise the capital to expand. This was dismaying news, for I sensed that no one had worked harder than McAuliffe. New Albion's passing was like the death of a prophet.

In the middle of receiving these mixed reports, I helped to found a brewpub, and it didn't cost me a dime. One day, while at work in the legislature, I got a call from Greg Noonan in Massachusetts. I recognized the name from the fine technical manual he had written on making lager beer. He wanted to build a brewpub in Vermont, probably in Burlington, but he needed the law changed to permit it. Could I help?

"Sure," said I, happy to work on something besides banking regulation and a gathering battle between the state and the electric power industry.

Existing laws, passed after Prohibition, prohibited "tied-houses" or brewery-owned bars, the general practice in England. These laws required a three-tiered system of brewery, distributor, and retailer. Vermont law said that no second-class licensee—that is, someone who sells beer for off-premise consumption—could also make the beer.

Knowing that there were usually several ways to skin a legislative cat, we turned the problem upside down. What if a brewery (manufacturer) could have a retail license to sell beer on its premises? After a certain amount of drafting acrobatics, that idea found favor with the Liquor Control Board, and then progressively with four legislative committees, both legislative chambers, and finally the governor. In late 1988, Noonan's Vermont Pub and Brewery opened its doors (and taps). He asked me to cut the ribbon. Burlington had its first brewery in ninety-four years.

Maybe that was satisfaction enough—to be the legislative father to a brewpub. But that experience juiced me up again. With Jim Hinkel's cautionary notes in mind, I took another look.

As the Greeks said 2,500 years ago, "Know thyself!" The first question was obviously: Why do I want to do this?" As Alan Davis of Catamount said, "Is it current job dissatisfaction? A desire to brew the world's best beer? An irresistible entrepreneurial urge? Upon reflection, is it reasonable to expect microbrewing will satisfy these needs? The start-up will be a lot longer and harder than you suspect."

What to brew was paradoxically complex. The big difference between the homebrewer and the microbrewer is that, whereas the former makes what he likes, the latter must *sell* what he makes. For Professor Michael Lewis, it is not enough for a prospective brewer to say, "I want to make a beer *like* Heineken's or Sierra Nevada or Stoudt's Maerzen." The brewer must believe that his is the best possible beer he can produce, for that faith is imperative in elbowing out the dozens of competing brands.

What format would I choose—microbrewery, brewpub, or contract brewing? Each had its pros and cons. Did I really want to run a restaurant as well as a brewery? Sam Adams' founder Jim Koch went the contract route and scoffed at the "edifice complex" of one's own brewery. "From the business standpoint, it makes no sense to build a brewery. The beer is not going to be cheaper and it's not going to be better."

I would have to learn a lot more practical professional brewing.

73

Would I go back to school? Would I try to work 70 hours a week for slave wages at an existing brewery? Would that get me the necessary skills? Jack McAuliffe said, "Brewing means turning water into money." The brewer who starts from scratch must be a hybrid of pack rat, junk dealer, shade-tree mechanic, and surgeon who slavers over food-equipment magazines the way others do over *Playboy*. When I asked Jim Schleuter of River City what skills I would need, he said, "Electrical work, plumbing, welding, tile work, carpentry, refrigeration, practical biology, mechanical ability, and all-purpose cussing. Much of it must be in the blood. By the time you're an adult, you don't have time to learn all these things." At the same time, it helped to have what Paul Camusi of Sierra Nevada called "that indefinable feel for brewing."

After spending several years developing beer formulas, raising money, finding a location, scrounging for equipment, and living on macaroni and cheese, the new brewer might be forgiven for believing that the beer will be an instant success—without marketing.

Next comes regulation. Beer is a regulated drug. Like it or not, when you make and distribute beer, federal, state, and local officials have a special interest in you and your work. If you don't like regulations and rules, you probably shouldn't be brewing for a living.

The federal Alcohol, Tobacco, and Firearms Bureau is primarily interested in your criminal record and your readiness to pay a per-barrel federal tax.

Every state has its own alcohol regulatory agency. The brewer must also please the state in other matters, such as health and employment codes, manufacturers' fees, etc. Local authorities oversee zoning and building permits.

And then there were the costs! They were the *coup de grace* for my brewery dreams.

Newman and Reich each raised an initial $250,000, but they spent it in dramatically different ways. Newman channeled his money into a building and brewing equipment, whereas Reich put every extra cent over the cost of his contract with F. X. Matt into marketing.

To give a *rough* idea of how much a four-to-six-thousand-barrel freestanding brewery would cost in 1994, I turned to Lawrence Miller of Otter Creek Brewing. Although he assembled his brewery for considerably less, he estimated the costs at $300,000-400,000. If you sell what you make, you will earn a living wage, at least initially. This did not include a bottling line—which could add anywhere from $50,000 to $200,000—or real-estate/rental costs.

Whew! In the end, I realized I had no more business in commercial brewing than I had in professional bag-piping, or full-time beekeeping, or running marathons every couple of weeks. I could not raise that amount of money for a real try at success. I was pretty sure I didn't have the mechanical skills to run pumps and bottling lines. I was probably not conscientious enough to maintain the operating-room cleanliness needed to make uncontaminated beer month after month.

The words of Michael Lewis came back to me: "The ones who make it in this business will be extreme characters. The work is extraordinarily hard, and those that don't give it one hundred percent won't get to first base. This is a seven-day job if you build from scratch. To be successful, the microbrewer must have a *savage commitment* to every aspect of brewing and selling. For every hundred people who think about building a brewery, ten may try it and only one will succeed."

Finally, as Fritz Maytag warned, "To be a brewer, you must have nightmares regularly. You've got to think about problems all the time."

For me, it was home to homebrew. Deciding not to build a brewery simplified my life and allowed me to take uncomplicated pleasure in the hobby of homebrewing. True, I was using more complex equipment—wort chiller, propane stove, and kegs—and brewing more elaborate beers. But brewing was again a comfortable, predictable, manageable pursuit, which left time for my other hobbies of beekeeping, running, fly-fishing—and more time for my family. Like the farmer adjusting to the seasons, I could brew six to eight times a year, drink one or two glasses of an evening, and give the rest away.

And then came along a certain beekeeping brewer named Todd Haire.

During one of my trips to Magic Hat for a growler of beer (a luxury I allowed myself during my semi-retirement from homebrewing after 1994), I chatted up an acquaintence who was pulling taps. He told me that the head brewer, Todd Haire, was also a beekeeper. "Go on back and introduce yourself!" he urged. I made my way through a forest of fermentation vessels and pallets of beer stacked to the ceiling.

Todd turned out to be warm, funny, and easy-going—even with the intensity of brewing seven days a week. His only demerit was his love of the New York Yankees. We hit it off. I would answer his beekeeping questions, and he could easily handle my brewing questions. It turned out we were both looking for a new place for a beeyard: He was plagued by bears and I had incompetent beekeepers crowding my space.

Todd got his boss's approval to let us put six hives on a berm behind the brewery. I loved the setup because I could stop off there on my way home from work to check the bees, and pick up a growler in the process. Over the next three to four years, the system worked well. Todd brewed an experimental beer, a braggot, with honey and chamomile. He used about thirty pounds of our shared honey and got the rest from the Champlain Valley Apiaries in Middlebury. It made me feel, momentarily, like a professional brewer.

❧ 8 ❧

Beer is a Beast

by Todd Haire

It's the fall of 2012, and I'm driving my noisy Jeep down Flynn Avenue toward Switchback Brewing Company in Burlington, Vermont. Through the trees, I can see Lake Champlain and the Adirondack mountains. Today will be fun: We will be dumping three-to-four hundred gallons of beer down the drain.

There are two good times to dump beer. One is when you're testing new equipment—like we will be today. We'll be running the beer through our new bottle filler to test the quality of the fill. We'll test for dissolved oxygen and air pick-up in this process. (Oxygen in beer will destroy its fresh flavor faster than you can chug a can. So we will tweak, adjust, and test over and over again until we are satisfied with the results.) The other time to dump beer is when the batch is "off" for any number of reasons. You do *not* sell bad beer.

Making consistently great beer is a never-ending obstacle course. As a brewer, you've got to think of the beer all the time—not just when you're in the brewery. Beer has everything going against it until it is enjoyed.

Other questions come to mind as I drive: How will the micro-plating look this week for bacteria and wild yeast counts? Are the fermentations trending correctly? Will the spent grain auger that removes the old mash be frozen again? Will the hot, humid day that's predicted for today affect our bottling fill volumes or labeling machine?

As I get out of the Jeep, I get a rich complex mixture of smells. The sweet, cereal-grain aroma from the mash joins the sharp hoppiness from the wort boil in the kettle. It is a distinctive aroma that you either love or hate. I find it quite nice. (If you are ever outside at the Newark airport in New Jersey and the wind direction is correct, you can smell the wort from the Budweiser brewhouse just a few miles away. It overwhelms the odors of marshlands, chemical plants, and jet fuel.)

When I walk into the brewery and greet Tony Morse, the lead brewer, the fruity carbonic smell of fermenting beer is just right. The music is just right, too. Coltrane simmers like a pre-boiling kettle before an explosive crescendo. Music in our brewery is as important as coffee. It sets the tone, and anyone working can choose it. Our selection has evolved from dusty stacks of compact discs to iPods set to shuffle and playlists streaming from online apps. If anyone is feeling nostalgic, there is a box of Grateful Dead and '80s New Wave cassette tapes. Music puts a good vibe in the air to start the day.

As Head Brewer/Operations Manager at Switchback, I oversee the production and quality of the beer from brewhouse to package. Luckily, we are a small, dedicated crew of brewers here. Today, everyone is busy with daily work: connecting hoses to pumps, measuring gas volumes in tanks, hauling bags of malt for milling, weighing out hops for brews. Rubber brewers' boots and gloves line the wall like bats and mitts in a baseball dugout. The sights, the smell, and the sounds of the brewery are in full swing. Everyone is in good spirits, and I can feel it. It gets livelier as the day progresses and we test the bottle filler.

In an adjoining room stand pallets piled with sacks of malted barley from the U.S., England, Germany, Belgium, and Canada, with specialty ingredient names of Pale, Crystal, Cara Pils and Black. Next to them are rows of empty, stainless steel keg cooperage wrapped in plastic, waiting to be filled. The racking machine for keg filling is not far away. Our ten-gallon pilot brewery stands ready for the next experimental brews.

In one sense, a brewery is just a big circulatory system, moving beer around like the body moves blood. To support this movement is the mechanical side. I listen to the low drone of the boiler and the high pitch whine of the compressors delivering compressed air to pneumatic valves and cylinders. I listen to the confident clanging of hundreds of bottles being readied for the bottling line, 500 at a time. The stainless steel kegs add their own tinny baritone. Irregular whooshes come from the steam cleaner. And above it all, Coltrane.

I climb the stairs to the 1964 copper brewhouse, which our owner, Bill Cherry, purchased from a defunct brewery in Germany. The golden sheen is a brilliant contrast to the stainless steel of so many other tanks in the room. There is a noticeable dry heat here around the kettles. The brewhouse, with its mash mixer, is used to mix the grains with water and step through different temperature ranges to start developing the sweet liquid called wort. The mash is then pumped slowly over to the lauter tun, which is much like a large sieve (*lautern* means "to clarify" in German) that clarifies the wort of large and small grain fractions by recirculating it through the grain bed. When the wort is clear, it is then slowly pumped over to the boiling kettle. When I once visited an English brewery, a brewer told me if he saw his reflection in the liquid in the mash, he knew that the wort had converted from starch to sugar and was ready to run off to the boiling kettle.

The grains are rinsed of sugar with hot water in the lauter tun until the boiling kettle volume is achieved. A vigorous rolling boil continues for over ninety minutes. During this process, the hops are added at different times to unite the sweet wort and bitter hops for balance. The last tank in the four that make up the brewhouse configuration is the whirlpool. The whirlpool helps separate the coagulated proteins, hop, and grain particles carried over in the process. The wort composition is then cooled and sent by pipe to a fermenter.

It's hot up here in the brewhouse year-round—not to mention in the summer. It's not uncommon for temperatures to reach 110 degrees, even in Vermont. Therefore, brew days start early and at times can run late. And here, in this hotbed, is where a brewer can often conjure up a new beer. You dream of colors, taste and balance of a particular beer. It could be emulating a beer you've just tried. Or you could want to develop flavor interpretations for pairing the beer with certain foods.

Other times you want to experiment with creating a mood from certain ingredients. ("How great would this beer taste with a porchetta sandwich?")

If we can indulge the analogy to the human body and see the brewhouse as the brain of the brewery, then the fermentation cellar is its heart and soul. The fermentation cellar, where the beer is aged, is my favorite part of the brewery. It's alive and standing in it, at times, can feel as if you're visiting a holy kind of stainless Stonehenge.

Although all the fermentation tanks are completely closed at Switchback, I have always enjoyed watching beer ferment in open tanks that reveal the process of changing the wort into beer. Such open fermentation is a tangible way of predicting the outcome of the fermentation beyond the microbiological side. Post fermentation, the yeast is floating on top of the new beer, and it is skimmed with stainless steel buckets from the top of the fermenter. A small sample is taken to check the viability, vitality and purity of the yeast via microscope. The yeast slurry, which has a very fruity/hoppy resinous taste and aroma, is then weighed out and pumped (or "pitched") into a fermenter based on the volume of wort. It's like having a dinner party where you want to have the right amount food for the right amount of people. Not too much, not too little. Some yeast strains (primarily ale yeast) used over generations of brews start to acclimate to the fermentation environment they are subjected to. The yeast strain can flourish or evolve over time to create a beautiful house character in the beer unlike anyone else. The yeast becomes the fingerprint of that beer.

After the cooled wort is aerated in-line by porous rods and delivered to the fermenter from the brewhouse, it sits quietly for a few hours. The yeast is now taking up oxygen and reproducing. Then there is a slow movement of swirling gas bubbles rising through the visible wort. A layer of cappuccino-like froth appears over the wort and starts to grow. This is "low krausen." The engine of fermentation has begun.

Over the next several hours, the fermentation will build to its peak. The foam will rise up the straight wall of the vessel and, at times, bubble over the top. This is known as "high krausen." It is a beautiful sight—like watching great billowy cumulus cloud formations. There is energy here. If you hold your hand over the foam you can feel the warmth generated by the fermentation and you can see the carbon-dioxide vapor hovering above the rim of the tank. The surface looks like the top of a meringue pie, with its golden waves and its specks of proteins and hop resin.

As the fermentation settles, the fresh ale yeast that has risen to the top is skimmed, or "harvested." In our small lab, we test the yeast and, if healthy, use it for subsequent brews. After the yeast has been skimmed, the tank will later be cooled and the remaining yeast will settle down to create a protective cap over the beer. Now, that cap looks like a cross cut section of the human brain or a big bowl of noodles.

Soon after this, the beer is cooled and begins to go through its aging process. During the maturation time, condensation drips from the sides of tanks that have been chilled to near freezing temperatures. The cold temperatures are made possible by highways of cooling lines full of propylene glycol, leading to and away from tanks. This coolant is pumped though a jacket that surrounds the fermentation tank and helps to maintain fixed temperatures during primary fermentation. Again, it's hard not to think of the brewery as having its own living, pumping circulatory system. In the fermentation cellar, it's easy to get lost in reverie. I often find myself recalling the words of past teachers and thinking back on my brewing career. Today is no exception…

Brewers generally come from two backgrounds—the artistic or scientific side. I originally came from the artistic side and then learned the scientific. Brewing is an expression of all your senses. It is something I learned from my father-in-law, Mario Lubic. Without realizing it, I got some of my brewing knowledge and philosophy from watching him make beautiful wine and grappa. His technique was based on years of knowledge, practice, and experimentation. He could determine grape sugar content not with a refractometer, but by touch and taste. He would know the essence of temperature and time for fermentation and maturation in barrels by adjusting the cellar window, not by using temperature control cooling apparatuses. Mario taught me about how the weather and the humidity affected the wine. Working with him, I learned the importance of the hands-on approach—you need to know *why* you are doing what you are doing and how every action affects the outcome.

I wish that I could have worked with a mentor of Mario's status earlier in my brewing career. It was really hard to find guidance when I started brewing. There was not a deep community of experienced, knowledgeable small craft brewers to consult with—and no internet. I had to learn the technical side in the early days through trial and error, slow adjustments for improvement, a lot of reading, and by asking a lot of questions. Some year later, I had the opportunity to brew for two weeks under the supervision of the late Master Brewer Dr. Joseph Owades, who had helped Matthew Reich, and epitomized the scientific approach. Mario epitomized the art. But brewing has to be a balance of both.

I was born in Houston, Texas, and raised just outside Dallas in the then quiet town of Plano in late '70s and early '80s. My father was a travelling salesman for Beckton Dickinson who sold pharmaceutical supplies to hospitals. He was on the road two to three weeks out of the month. This left my patient mother to take care of my brother and me. Like most boys, we were little hellions at times. But by nature, I was quiet and enjoyed doing things on my own. In school, I was average. I enjoyed classes where I could create something—small engine repair, metal shop, and wood shop. Like my father, I enjoyed working with my hands and exploring how things work. In those days, you were shunned if you were in tech. And not playing football made me doubly shunned.

Other than that, I had a pretty normal childhood. When not in school, I spent most of my time outside. We lived near a lake and I spent my time fishing for crayfish and turtle hunting, being careful not to arouse a water moccasin. I could not know then I would become a brewer, so it is ironic that one of my hobbies was collecting beer cans. Besides the ones my father would bring home from business trips (like Schlitz, Schmidt's, Pearl and Lone Star) were those my brother and I picked up searching the woods, ditches and dumps for hidden gold. I think in the end we had about 300 different cans.

My other hobby was music. We listened to a lot of music. After wearing my mother down, she finally traded in my brother's dusty clarinet for a guitar and lessons for me.

In 1984, my father's company transferred him to northern New Jersey. I was midway through high school. Suddenly, I no longer wore cowboy boots, had to quickly learn to stop saying "y'all," and rejoiced that corporal punishment was prohibited in the North. Soon, my brother and I and a few of our new friends would spend our weekends taking the train to New York, getting into trouble and having a couple of Prior Double Darks at Mona's on 14th and Avenue B.

The city was alive with music that I loved. There was punk from the Big Boys and Scratch Acid, and bands like the Bad Brains and Minutemen. We would get records at Bleeker Bob's on Bleeker Street in Greenwich Village or hit Pier Platters Records in Hoboken. We would wait until our various favorite bands toured and go see them once a year. The shows were usually a Sunday matinee at CBGB's. The music resonated with me and I wanted that feeling constantly.

In my final year of high school, it seemed as if everyone around me was heading to college. Not me. I struggled to find something I was seriously interested in, and I didn't think college would help me find it. I remember having an honest conversation with my father about my dilemma. He was very understanding and told me to work it out my own way, and he would support me in whatever direction I took.

My father had always stressed that listening was more important than talking. His advice taught me to learn skills quickly and correctly, because there wasn't much room for error. "Be safe, be aware and do it correctly the first time." This has stuck with me to this day.

In the summer of 1991, my father was diagnosed with cancer. It spread so quickly that he died within three months. It was a tough time for our family and a harsh life lesson. We all dealt with the surreal fact of his death in separate ways. I quit my job and spent my time not thinking for a while. It was my friends at the time who really helped me through this period of my life. They would come over and we would play music in the house we rented. None of us had much going on, but the music allowed us to be creative. We became a three-piece band, doing what we thought was avant-guard stuff. We started playing small shows and somehow convinced a small label to record our music. We recorded four songs in Brooklyn.

We traveled up and down the east coast playing shows at bars and colleges, drinking beer, and crashing on people's floors for the night. We made just enough money playing music and selling T-shirts to keep the van rolling. But after a year or so, the gigs were not showering us with riches. At least in a traditional sense...

Then I met Monica at one of our weekend shows. In 1992, we were playing at a bar in Cambridge, Massachusetts, called The Middle East. A mutual friend introduced me to Monica, and we've been together ever since. She had just started graduate school and was working at an automotive warehouse in Alston where she lived at the time. Since I knew quickly that she was the best thing that ever happened to me, over the next year I took a lot of round-trip bus rides from the Port Authority to Boston. When she finished grad school, Monica moved to New Jersey and began teaching at a small alternative school in Jersey City. I started a new day job at the Grand Opening Liquor Store in Haledon.

At this time, our portfolio of beer drinking was limited by the size of our wallet. We tried a handful of imports like Watney's Red Barrel and McEwan's Scotch Ale. Guinness and Bass seemed to be on tap everywhere. Yuengling was a favorite and was cheaper by the dozen. Looking back, my beer odyssey truly began there at the Grand Opening. This is where I began to really think about how great beer was made, its variety, and why it tasted the way it did. My interest was piqued by the guys who ran the store—Chris Schiavo and his brother in-law Mike Perini. They were passionate about beer. They thought of themselves as the Jack Kerouac and Neal Cassady of beer. (Chris now owns the Shepard and the Knucklehead: a craft beer bar in Haledon, New Jersey, that boasts many great beers.)

As the beer buyer and manager of the store, Chris and Mike would bring in hundreds of beers—both imports from everywhere and many of the craft beers that were emerging around the U.S. It felt like a world's fair of beer; I couldn't get enough. Two craft beers I enjoyed the most at the time were both from Pennsylvania: Red Feather Ale and Stoudt's Brewing. Stoudt's was packaging an assortment of styles in 765 ml. green bottles. I loved buying them to share with Monica. Trying all the different styles of beer was exciting. We loved their beer so much we made a weekend trip to Adamstown, Pennsylvania, to spend a weekend drinking beer and watching country line dancing in their amazing beer hall. (An odd pairing made more interesting by the beer and ambience.)

Chris and Mike were my first beer mentors. They urged me to read books on beer and taught me to appreciate good beer. They would load me up with a six pack of different beers each weekend and say, "Go home, try them and write about them. You don't know what you think until you write it down." They taught me that you interact with beer not just with your mouth, but also with your brain.

We went on field trips, too. We visited the Old Town Bar in Union Square, whose most memorable feature was a urinal the size of a coffin. We went to Chumley's, the literary bar in the East Village of the Beat Generation. How cool it was to sit and have a beer next to an open fireplace! We went to McSorley's, with those signature offerings of two mugs: "Light or Dark!" We even drove up to Albany to Mahar's Public Bar to try their incredible beer selection.

Twice every year we would attend the Beers International beer dinner put on by the late beer impresario Richie Stolarz. Every year Richie would invite his friend Michael Jackson—the most famous beer writer in the world—to visit, taste, and write about new breweries and beer in New York and New Jersey. Jackson talked about the beer that was paired with the food. I would take notes of what Michael tasted and revisit the beer another night to compare what he tasted and what I tasted. This really helped me understand the descriptive vocabulary of beer connoisseurship.

In '93, my brother Tim and I decided to try homebrewing. We looked at several books, like the first edition of *Making Beer* by Bill Mares and *The Beginner's Home Brew Book* by Lee Coe, but they weren't technical enough. Then we bought Charlie Papazian's book *The Joy of Home Brewing*, and we didn't look back.[1] The only problem was that many of the ingredients he talked about weren't available to us. The closest home-brew store was in Teaneck, about twenty miles away. It didn't have much variety and was only open very irregular hours.

So we improvised. We'd grab a few of the ingredients, throw them in a bucket, and see how it turned out. It was mostly dry or liquid malt,

---

1 When I was at Magic Hat, Charlie Papazian came to visit. I told him how enjoyable it was to host him because I had gotten my start in brewing with his book. A year later Charlie sent me his new book called Microbrewed Adventures. I was so excited and honored to be mentioned in the book. I wrote to him to say, "Ten years ago I was reading your book about *you* brewing beer, and now I'm reading your book about *me* making beer!"

packaged yeasts—very primitive. From Charlie's book, we brewed Toad Spit Stout and Cherries in the Snow (but substituted raspberries instead). We brewed a Dark Winter Clove Ale and called it "Is it Safe?", a reference to the Dustin Hoffman movie, Marathon Man. But mostly we made English bitter ales with varying amounts of hops. We retrofitted a refrigerator to start pouring our favorite craft beers and homebrew on tap. The kegs at the time were all Hoff Stevens', the round belly bung style with a two-prong tap. We would go down the road to the Boylan's birch beer shop where they made and filled draught birch beer on Lee Avenue to get the keg supplies we needed, like carbon-dioxide gas, keg bungs, and tap gaskets. After several homebrew batches, I was hooked. But I decided I wanted more complexity in the beers and more understanding of the craft brewing process.

Month at Siebel

Late in 1994, I was talking to Monica about our future and how beer fit in. I didn't want to work at the beer store for the rest of my life, and I wasn't good enough at music to play forever. Since making beer was something I felt passionate about, I wondered if maybe I should try getting into that industry. Without hesitation, Monica said "Go for it!" And so it was settled.

I knew I needed some formal education well beyond homebrewing and also something that would stand out on a paper resume if a brewing opportunity arose. From time to time, an avid and excellent homebrewer named Jim Salmon would come into the liquor store and we would talk about homebrewing. He would give me bottles of his latest brews and we would talk shop about brewing and all the new beer that had come in. During one of our conversations he said he was going to take a short course in brewing at a place called The Siebel Institute of Technology in Chicago. Jim didn't intend to become a professional brewer, but he did want to get a better understanding about brewing from a classroom perspective.

I sent for and received a catalog from Siebel. They offered an intensive two-week short course in Brewing Technology in the classroom, and, after that, a two-week apprenticeship at a Chicago brewery or brew pub. The staff instructors at Siebel were fifteen legends in the field of brewing. The short course covered everything from Barley and Malting with master maltster Kurt Duecker, to Brewhouse Operations with Brewmaster Walter "Swiss" Swistowicz, to Yeast Physiology with Dr. Joe Power, and on and on. What's more, the tuition covered lunch and beer. That would be a lot of bratwurst and Old Style beer. The least expensive option for a place to stay was at the "Leaning Tower YMCA," which even had a shuttle to Siebel.

I applied, and in March of 1995 was admitted to the fiftieth short course in Brewing Technology. From the start, I loved the experience. Siebel has a motto that has stuck with me: "Not only do we teach our students, but we also help them to teach each other." There were about twenty people in my class from all around the country. Most were from breweries, but some were trade people—the most notable being Brad Coors from Coors Brewing Co. He rolled with all the banter from the new small craft brewers attending. The lectures were long and intense, but I sopped them up like a sponge. Two weeks in the classroom flashed by.

The two-week apprenticeship on a brewery floor that followed was a real eye opener. I chose to work in a production brewery called Chicago Brewing Co., which was housed in an old pickle factory on the West Side. When it opened in 1990, it was the first production brewery in Chicago in over fifty years.

The brewer at the time was Greg Moehn, a Siebel graduate of the diploma course. Greg has a rich family history in brewing. Greg's great uncle started the Moehn Brewing Co. in Burlington, Iowa, in the late 1800s.

The Chicago Brewing Co. brewery was cold, dark, and damp. Its machinery had been cobbled together and kept breaking down a lot, especially the bottling equipment. But that's the way it was in the early days of craft breweries. Most people were trying to build breweries on a shoestring budget with little off-the-shelf equipment. Most of the equipment had come from a large defunct brewery, and we had to be creative and inventive to make it work. That didn't matter much for me. Just walking around a real brewery with all the pipes, the steaming, the smells, the ideas of taking malt, water, yeast and hops and making beer was exciting. I was hooked, for sure.

At the end of the last week, Greg brought a few of us up to the roof of the brewery where we had a panoramic view of the Chicago downtown. We were drinking a few Legacy Lager and Big Shoulders Porter that we packaged that week. I remember thinking to myself that there was nothing better than drinking a beer at the end of the day, especially one that you had a hand in making. I still think that today.

Amazingly, in the first week after I got back from Siebel, I heard about a start-up brewery in Hoboken where we lived. It was called Mile Square Brewing Company (after the approximate size of the city) and was located at the old Maxwell House factory on the Hudson River looking across at Manhattan. The brewery was in one small area where the coffee cans had been made. This seemed like an incredible opportunity right on my doorstep, so I walked in and volunteered to work for free. At that pay, they were happy to hire me. I mopped, I scraped, I hauled bags of grain, I moved equipment, I painted, I did all the grunt work they needed done. After two months, I asked if I could get paid, and they agreed. There were only two paid employees: a former brewer from Rockies Brewing Co. in Boulder, Colorado, named Mike Gilmore, and me.

The brewery consisted of a new twenty-barrel system (Diversified Metal Engineering), six forty-barrel fermenters, two forty-barrel bright beer tanks, a small bottle filler from Italy, and a stockpile of old belly bung Hoff Steven kegs. The kegs had an opening on the side for removing the wooded bung. We would take out the bung to clean it with a drill press to release the gas.

One of my most vivid memories from Mile Square was the day we pressurized our bright beer tank during our first beer transfer. We had close to thirty barrels of beer in the packaging/bright tank. The pressure in the tank was about ten pounds per square inch when the manway door gasket started to leak. As we tightened down the door, the leak increased to a large spray. Just as I stepped to the side of the tank the manway door blew off the tank and flew twenty yards out into the brewery followed by a freakish horizontal column of beer flying from the tank. Someone standing in front of this artillery round would have been badly injured. Fortunately, no one was, and we spent the next three hours squeegeeing beer to the drain. (It turned out that the manway door was slightly smaller than the manway.)

Shortly after the brewery was truly up and running, the owners fired Mike. Now I was doing everything: brewing, transferring, and filtering—with only six months' worth of experience. We were brewing about 800 barrels a year. Looking back, it was a bit crazy there. They didn't seem to have a very good business plan. The pay was not very good, but, then again, neither was my experience to be heading up a brewery.

After another six months, the owners of Mile Square hired two nationally renowned brewery consultants. One was Dr. Joseph Owades, the inventor of light beer and the man who had helped Samuel Adams develop its lager. The other was William H. Moeller, who helped Brooklyn Lager get rolling.

Dr. Owades' contract was to help the brewery develop some new styles. Even though I had only been brewing for a few months, I got to brew right next to him. The first thing he said we needed was a microscope and a stir plate. He taught me the importance of yeast cell counts, of pitch rates for fermenters, and of a rapid fermentation test to show the nuances of how mash profiles affect the finished beer. We brewed a Black Wit with coriander and orange that was unheard of at the time and spiced brown ale with fenugreek.

All I wanted was to learn more and more. The answer to every question I asked him prompted twenty more questions. I felt very fortunate to spend time with Owades in the brewery. I didn't want to waste a minute with him. It was like having the whole Siebel Institute at my side every day. But instead of trying the adventuresome beers, we started making two simple, inoffensive styles of beer: Mile Square Amber Ale and Mile Square Golden Ale.

After a year in Hoboken, I began feel like I needed to look for other opportunities. The brewing community was surely growing and I had hundreds of questions, but no one to answer them where I worked. I started attending informal brewers' guild meetings in Manhattan. These were the brain child of the generous Garrett Oliver, the brewmaster at Brooklyn Brewery. Before Brooklyn, Garrett had been the brewmaster at Manhattan Brewing. He began inviting brewers from around the New York area to gather quarterly at Brooklyn Brewery, The Telephone Bar in NYC, or a fellow brewer's brewery. We would have a social hour and then follow up with a technical presentation from Garrett or a guest brewer/speaker. One speaker was Sam Calagione who had just opened Dogfish Head in Delaware. Another was the original brewmaster at Wynkoop's, Russell Schehrer. Tragically, Schehrer later died in a fall at his Brooklyn apartment. (For his incredible contribution to brewing education, the Brewers Association created the Russell Scherer Award for Innovation in Craft Brewing.) These guild meetings were great mixture of learning and sharing experiences in a comfortable setting.

In that next year, two more breweries opened in the New York area. They were Heartland Brewery in Union Square and Commonwealth Brewing in Rockefeller Center. There I got to know Paul Sayler, who had worked in Vermont at Catamount Brewing for five years before coming down to NYC to be the head brewer at Commonwealth. Imagine putting in a brewery right there on 5th Avenue! I thought to myself, *maybe that's the next place I should try?*

But I took a detour back to Siebel instead. At one of the brewers' meetings in 1996, Garrett told me that the American Institute of Wine and Food was offering a two-month scholarship to Siebel called the Michael Jackson Beer Education Scholarship, sponsored by Brooklyn Beer Co. I thought *What the heck, I'll apply.* It would give me a chance to deepen my formal brewing knowledge. I wrote an essay, and was interviewed by Steve Hindy, owner of Brooklyn Brewery. I won the scholarship to attend the Diploma Course in Brewing Technology during the fall of 1997.

I told the Mile Square brewery owners that this was a terrific opportunity, and that I would bring back lots of information to make better beer. I also asked for a raise when I returned because it was hard to live on $6.00 an hour. Their response was a spit in the face. No, really—a spit in the face. I turned in my keys and never looked back. As luck would have it, I was offered a job by Jim Migliarini, head brewer at Heartland Brewing in Union Square. I was able to go to Siebel knowing I would have a job when I returned.

The ten weeks at Siebel were exactly what I'd hoped for. The course was intense and difficult. We lived and breathed beer—from both the science and the sensory end. We had labs, weekly quizzes, a midterm and a final. The classes on sensory analysis and threshold tastings were my favorite. I loved learning about the development of flavors in beer, positive and negative.

One of the course requirements was to make a beer from start to finish. I worked with Mark Henion (currently the head brewer at the Boneyard Brewery in Bend, Oregon) and Jeff Hobkins (currently a brewer at Guinness in Ireland) on this project. It required malting barley; developing a recipe using brewing formulations for malt bill, hopping rates, and water usage; and brewing it on a small pilot system. It was a pale ale that we named Haggis.

The people at Siebel were as inspiring as ever. There were brewers from around the world; there were Anheuser-Busch and Miller people as well as craft brewers. Nobody was arrogant. I still stay in contact with some of the students I studied with, and although my library of brewing books has grown, my beat-up binders from Siebel are the most important books on my brewery shelf.

When I returned from the course, I began to work at Heartland Brewing in Union Square. I knew what it was like to work in a production brewery, but I wanted to add the experience of a brewpub. Every day, I travelled into NYC wearing shorts and a T-shirt while everyone else on the train was wearing a suit.

In the brewpub, I felt like I was making beer in a kitchen. It was a restaurant first and a brewery second: I milled grain next to the guy peeling potatoes. All of our malt had to come two floors down to the basement. It arrived on pallets with a thousand 55-pound bags. Getting rid of the spent grain was a chore in itself. It's never easy to move things around in New York City; I give a lot of credit to people who do it. Of all those early Manhattan breweries, I think Heartland is the only one still around.

After six months there, Monica and I began to think about moving. Paul Sayler had been keeping me apprised of jobs in New England breweries, and one day he called to say that both Tremont Brewery in Boston and Magic Hat in Burlington were looking for brewers. I applied for both jobs. Within days I got a call from Bob Johnson, the vice-president of Magic Hat.

I had my interview with Bob at the original 15-barrel brewery on Flynn Avenue. Bob was a former cheesemaker at Shelburne Farms and an avid homebrewer with the Green Mountain Mashers homebrewing club. Magic Hat's brewhouse consisted of a wooden clad mash/lauter tun and a direct gas-fired brew kettle. The hot-water tank for brewing was the salvaged back end of a dairy milk truck fit up with a heater element and legs. The fermentation tanks were a mix of fifteen to thirty barrel, open top vessels and a reclaimed rectangular shallow cheese vat for separating curd from the whey.

Magic Hat was in the process of moving to a new site, and the new spot near a lumberyard had plenty of space to grow. In contrast to the original brewery, this one was first class. The brewhouse was a 50-barrel size from a leading manufacturer in Oregon. Magic Hat would soon start bottling all its beer on site with a mechanical filler that ran at one hundred bottles per minute. What fun it would be to work here!

After the tour of the brewery we went downtown to meet up with

Alan Newman, the visionary guru of Magic Hat, at a Burlington bar called the Chicken Bone. Alan had a quick wit and a way of asking off-beat questions to get a feel for someone's personality and drive. Over a few beers, he pressed me with variations of "Why in the world would you ever want to move to Vermont and make beer?" My first answer was that I enjoyed the beers. I also loved that Burlington had interesting art and music—it felt like Hoboken, but on a smaller (and colder) scale.

Two weeks later, just after I returned from the Craft Brewers Conference in Atlanta, Bob called to say I was hired. I was thrilled. As it turns out, it was doubly lucky that I didn't try for the Tremont Brewery job in Boston. Tremont closed three years later! When I started at Magic Hat in April, 1998, I was one of four brewers who brewed 6,000 barrels per year. When I left in 2010, there were twelve brewers brewing over 180,000 barrels per year and we were the ninth-largest craft brewery in the country.

We had a great team of brewers during those years. In addition to myself, there was Matt Cohen, who is now the owner and brewer of Fiddlehead Brewing Company in Shelburne, Vermont. There was Andrew Hagedorn, who came to us while attending the University of Vermont, and would later leave for the UC Davis Brewing School and move on to New Belgium in Fort Collins. And there was John Ravell, who became production manager and is now working again with Alan Newman at his company, Alchemy and Science.

The four of us did all the brewing, filtering, and keg racking. We communicated almost instinctively. Those years were good but very lean. The brewery was growing like crazy—almost 25-30 percent a year. In 2000, I was promoted to the head brewer job, directly under Bob Johnson. When Bob left in 2002, I became Head of Brewery Operations, or in the crazy nomenclature we developed, the "Lead Technician of Supernatural Assembly and Huge Growth."

During my years at Magic Hat, we were brewing an ale which became "Bob's 1st," "#9" (the apricot-flavored beer which became our flagship brand), "Heart of Darkness," "Jinx," "Hocus Pocus," and "Blind

Faith." We were always experimenting—that's what Alan wanted. We didn't have a true pilot system, so we brewed on a large scale. We felt confident knowing how the recipes would work on that level and we were let loose to brew what we thought was unique.

One beer that stands out in my mind was a barley wine we produced called Chaotic Chemistry. It was aged in bourbon barrels for three years. As soon as it was bottled, Alan wanted to put something else in the barrels. He jumped at the idea of an imperial stout I had brewed at my house. Our Humdinger Series was born. It consisted of Chaotic Chemistry, Thumbsucker (the imperial stout), and Braggot—a beer made with honey from the hives I kept outside of the brewhouse with Bill Mares. The flavors melded together perfectly and we put the beer into used white wine barrels. This was my first experience with barrel aging. One of the last barrel-aged beers we tried was a couple of mixed fermentation sour beers called Antioxidant Acid Ales. These draft-only beers were blended with blueberries, raspberries, and pomegranate.

In many ways, Alan was ahead of his time: with all the different flavors he pushed for and for the barrel-aged beers. He even wanted to do a distillery at one point. From my standpoint, the years from 1998 to 2003 were the golden years at Magic Hat. We had a great group, and beer was our life. Alan gave the brew staff carte blanche to try whatever we wanted. In return, we would do anything for that brewery. "Everyone" wanted to work at that brewery. There were talented, committed people throughout the whole organization; there was unbelievable energy and experimentation.

As the brewery grew, Alan would send a group of us around the country to look at other breweries our size to see how they handled pitfalls and challenges comparable to ours. Usually, the group included John Ravell, Matt Cohen, Steve Hood (General Manager), and myself. We traveled to Washington, Oregon, and Colorado.

Then at Craft Brewers Conferences, we would always take off a couple of days before or after and visit three or four breweries in that area. Most of what we discussed were qualitative things, such as centrifuges, bottle quality, brewhouse automation, and lab work. Steve Hood wanted to talk about the vendors of malts and hops. Being in the brewery talking one-on-one with the brewing staff was much better than listening to someone's PowerPoint presentation at the CBC. At the breweries, you could feel stuff and ask quick follow-up questions in a relaxed setting. We built up quite a network of people we'd see again and again.

There were also trips abroad. We traveled to Italy, Germany, and England. But the greatest trip was one I took to Belgium on my own time with a couple of Monica's relatives, Douglas Lubic and his son, Charles. I've always loved Belgian beers. At our wedding dinner in 1996, Monica and I served not Champagne, but Boon Kriek and Cantillon beers for toasts. Before the Belgium trip, I had only half-listened when Michael Jackson extolled Belgian beers as the most diverse and individualistic beers in the world. But then I learned how right he was. From the lambics to the guezes to the abbey beers, I learned for myself that Michael was spot-on when he said beers were to Belgium what cheeses were to France: "idiosyncratic, cranky and artisanal." We were drinking spontaneously fermented beers that pre-dated pitching of yeast.

We travelled to the Senne valley where lambic beer originated. We visited the Boon Brewery and got a tour from Frank Boon himself. (He has been making traditional lambic since 1978.) In the Ardennes region, we visited and got a tour of Orval—the Valley of Gold. I got to talk to Jean-Marie Rock, the head brewer, and told him that I had brewed an Orval clone from some of the yeast in the bottom of an Orval bottle. I said "Your beer is this high [gesturing to my head] and mine is this high [gesturing to my chest.]" Very politely, but insistently, he said, "My friend, I think your beer is down there." He was pointing to my knees. We laughed.

In West Flanders, where Scharabeek cherries come from, we visited a nineteenth century monastery brewery called Westvleteren. In downtown Brussels, we went to Cantillon's brewery where they make world-class lambic. At the top of the Cantillon building, there is a giant coolship—a shallow vessel for cooling wort. The coolship is open to the elements allowing the natural micro-flora to inoculate the wort as it cools. In Esen, we visited one of the quirkiest breweries—De Dolle. De Dolle is one of the beers that was part of my early beer education while working at the liquor store in New Jersey. Another highlight of the trip was walking along the oak barrels, or foeders, at Rodenbach in Roeselare. Being absorbed in the culture, the atmosphere, the landscape, and the wild beers of Belgium was phenomenal. The beers were so fresh. When we drink them here in the U.S., who knows how long they have travelled to get to us.

Back home, after my trip to Belgium, things were beginning to change at Magic Hat. The Brewery we all loved and were devoted to was getting bigger and bigger, and it was no longer the same. When the Brewery was sold to North American Brewers and Alan was no longer involved in the business, it was time for me to leave. I reached out to Switchback Brewing Company, a local brewery located in the same building complex where Magic Hat had started. They had grown steadily to become one of the most popular draft beers in Vermont. The timing was just right as they were looking to hire a Brewing Operations Manager.

Working at Switchback for the next four years was rewarding and fulfilling. I would stay at Switchback until I got the chance to start my own operation. Some of the things I most enjoyed while working at Switchback include building out the brewery lab, implementing a quality program, training staff in sensory analysis, and developing new beers. But most of all, it's the people who have made this brewery what it is. The dedicated Switchback staff are ready to take on the challenge of growth. I really enjoy that spirit and will take it with me wherever my brewing life leads. Oh, and the music—I always enjoy the music.

— *Todd*

⊱ 9 ⊰

Beer Hunting in Vermont

On a chill, overcast November morning in downtown Burlington in 2013, a hundred people gathered to honor Greg Noonan, the founder of the Vermont Pub and Brewery. Noonan, who died at the age of 52 of a fast-moving cancer, had been one of the giants of Vermont, and American, brewing. Author, counselor, and brewer, Noonan had both the foundational knowledge of brewing and the wisdom of how to explain it. He was a wonderful mentor and communicator. In 2005, as a tribute to his national influence, he was awarded the craft brewing industry's highest honor—the Russell Schehrer Award for Innovation in Brewing.

The actual event was held to install a plaque honoring the 25th anniversary of the Vermont Pub & Brewery, which Noonan had founded. Leading the festivities was Steve Polewacyk, Noonan's partner and his successor at Vermont Pub & Brew, or VPB. Among those in attendance were almost all of Greg's family and numerous friends from the Vermont brewing community. Fortuitously, the Vermont Brewers Association was having its annual meeting that weekend, just two blocks away. Its members came from all parts of the state. Some had known him well and had even worked for him. Others knew him only by reputation. A range of people gave eulogies. I spoke briefly about working together to get the brewpub law passed in the Vermont legislature in 1988. The VPB became Vermont's first brewpub and only the third on the East Coast.

As Todd and I moved among the guests, I mused about my faded desire to own a brewery. The closest I ever came was to cut the ribbon at the VPB's opening. Plenty of other people had stepped up. By 2013, there were over thirty-five breweries in Vermont—which made us the first or second state in the number of breweries per capita, competing with Oregon. (There were over 3,200 breweries nationwide.) Todd and I had joked before about starting our own brewery—a way to solidify a friendship and a passionate interest. But neither of us was ready to pull the proverbial trigger. Instead, we decided to do our own version of Michael Jackson's *Beer Hunter* and go look around.

The best person to start with was the voluble and articulate Lawrence Miller, who founded Otter Creek Brewing in 1991 and then sold it ten years later to Wolaver's of California. After working in several other businesses, he had become the commissioner of Economic Development for the State of Vermont. He was more than happy to meet us after work at the Three Penny Pub on Montpelier's Main Street, which specialized in craft beers from all over the U.S. and Europe.

With each of us drinking a different beer, Lawrence took a sip and launched into what could have been a prepared speech.

"The Vermont brewing industry was built on a great foundation. From the beginning, people wanted to make good beers. It has great people who shared knowledge, like Greg Noonan. He sold the first keg of beer I made. We also had early regulatory support. The state adapted to what we needed, without blowing open the door to create an unstable market. There was good camaraderie among all brewers—professionals and amateurs. The homebrewers were the educated consumers who could then educate the public to be more appreciative of good beer. The brewers benefited from these open-mouthed people willing to come back and say what they thought. If you were a brewer and open-minded you could adjust. Some who could not adjust, are not around anymore...."

"But what's the upper limit to the number of Vermont breweries?" I couldn't help asking.

Lawrence took another sip from his pint and sat back. "When we formed the Vermont Brewers Association (VBA) in 1994, I invited Steve Mason and Phil Gentile of Catamount, Andy Pherson of Long Trail, Alan Newman and Bob Johnson of Magic Hat, and some others to my house in Ripton. I roasted a leg of lamb. We cracked a jeroboam of Rodenbach to drink to the time when Vermont would have a beer culture like Belgium's. Maybe, we thought, that would come in fifty years. And then it happened in ten! We thought 10 percent of the Vermont market share for craft beers was the Holy Grail. Today, it's close to 20 percent! Now there are over forty brewers in state—I can't even keep track! No Vermont beer has a dominant market share. The beer culture has maintained its exploratory nature, even as the beers have gotten way more diverse than any of us ever expected."

From Montpelier, Todd and I went on to Middlebury to get another perspective from someone who has been both a brewer and a teacher of brewing at the American Brewers Guild—Steve Parkes, of the Drop-In Brewery. Parkes was trained as a brewer in England. He knew David Bruce of the Firkin empire of brew pubs, whom I had interviewed thirty years ago. He arrived in Woodland, California, to teach at the American Brewers Guild (ABG). After he bought the ABG, he changed its model to a teaching one. "We taught brewers how to teach, not teachers how to brew," said Parkes. He did so well that, like Greg Noonan, he won a Russell Schehrer Award.

"Vermont is farther along the path of community brewing because it's already a town-dominated state," Parkes asserted. "This is great for the beer freshness. The English have a good rule: 'Don't let beer travel further than a horse can travel in a day.'" As for the industry in general, Parkes was a bit more cautious: "It boggles my mind that someone could spend fifty-to-sixty-thousand dollars building a brewery with no professional experience whatsoever, and expect to be selling in the marketplace. Some brewers are coming from homebrewing and all their friends have told them they make the best beer in the world. You can't rely on your friends to evaluate your beer. I say do the professional test: Ask those same friends to *buy* your beer, and if they like it, to buy some more! Even if they have a good beer, distribution will be a chokepoint for new brewers. There's a finite number of taps, and the guys who have them aren't going to give them up. Vermont is becoming saturated with

breweries. There is only so much space on the grocery shelves."

Then it was up to Waterbury to see John Kimmich, owner with his wife Jen of the wildly successful Alchemist Brewery—the maker of Heady Topper. I was indebted to John for making a fabulous braggot for a big beekeeping conference I was running at the University of Vermont in 2012. John used about forty pounds of my honey to make two kegs with some special hops he had found. The first batch got washed away in the flood of 2011, but then, incredibly, John brewed another batch that we served at two evening events—to universal beekeeper approval. We asked John about a "Vermont brewing community."

"Well, yes, there's a brewers' community, as there is everywhere. The cream rises to the top, and if the brewers are reasonable, they are open and accepting of those that follow. People ask me, do you worry about a host of new brewers? I don't worry about that or anything else, except making my beer great! The rest will take care of itself.

"There are so many good beers out there, you have to be really good from the start. At the same time, people's palates are so different. Sometimes I'm shocked at what people call good beer. But every state has their great breweries, and every state has their duds." (John was in the middle of an expansion that would double his production to almost 20,000 barrels.)

Todd and I headed north. There are not many brewers who quote thinkers like Michel Foucault or Friedrich Nietzsche, and none who name a beer after the Danish philosopher Soren Kierkegaard's famous meditation *Fear and Trembling*. Shaun Hill lives right next to his hilltop brewery, part of a 200-year old family farm with a 360-degree view of Vermont's Northeast Kingdom. Like people on a religious retreat, the faithful and the novices trek up the hill to pay homage to Hill—and cash only for his exquisite range of beers. Many of the offerings are named after Hill's ancestors, such as "Arthur," "Susan," and "Harlan." Sometimes the line to purchase these stretches far out the door, and the line of cars on the drive is a quarter-mile long.

Shaun knew in high school that he wanted to be a brewer. After college, he worked in several U.S. breweries, then as a guest brewer in Belgium for three years. He returned to the family farm to start this brewery with equipment cobbled together from other Vermont brewers. In addition to the scores of pale ales and IPAs, he's also making small batches of mixed-culture beers. That he loved to do barrel-aged beers got our attention. According to Todd, Shaun makes some phenomenal saison beers, as good as anything he remembered from Belgium.

Vermont continued to fill up with breweries, and Todd and I continued to look around—toying all the while with the idea of a commercial enterprise of our own. New breweries dappled the state from Bennington to Lyndonville, from Brattleboro to St. Albans: Brewpubs, nanos and micros, all dreaming of being the next Alchemist, Lawson's, or Hill Farmstead. A few stood out. In Burlington, there was Queen City Brewery, where former Green Mountain Mashers Paul Hale, Maarten van Ryckevorsel, Paul Held, and Phil Kaszuba were brewing traditional lower-hopped beers, like Helles, Hefenweizen, Maibock, Yorkshire porter and Paul Hale's prize-winning steinbeer. In Winooski, there was Four Quarters where another former Masher and beekeeper Brian Eckert brewed an eclectic line of beers on a very small system. Ten miles north of glitzy Stowe, two brewers formerly from Trapp Brewing Company, Jamie Griffith and Allen Van Anda, took a triple chance: to resurrect an ancient beer style, brew it in the blue-collar town of Morrisville, and enter a town with an existing brewery. At Lost Nation, they make solid low alcohol, interesting beers like the Belgian saisons, a "Petit Ardennes," and the German Gose, made with salt and chamomile. Who would have thought that an almost-extinct German beer would become so popular in rural Vermont? "We wanted dry, clean, approachable brews," Van Anda said. "There is a niche for sessionable beer," he explained. They had an appealing tap room, and outside restaurant for the summer time.

"There's one more brewery we need to visit," Todd told me at the end of our circuitous route around the state. "It's down in Weston, and it's called Backacre. They make a very interesting lambic-style beer, very much on the Belgian model. It's a wild American ale, like those being brewed out West. These guys let the beer drive their schedule—not the reverse. The beer is ready when the beer is ready. Some like it, some hate it." We hit the road again.

Backacre is located in the hills above Weston on a farmstead owned by John Donovan, a retired dentist. Together with his daughter Erin and her husband, Matt, they began making the beer in 2008-'09. The couple got interested in sour beers when they spent two years in Belgium. Both have PhDs and work in Denver, Colorado. They travel back to Vermont twice a year to make beer, label it, and distribute it. Matt developed the recipe, and they brew 300 gallons of wort each time at a partner brewery. They drive it to their barn and pump it into the oak barrels with their yeast where it will sit and ferment for one to three years. They then bottle-condition the beer in 750 ml bottles for about two months. They only rinse the barrels out between fills. The barrels maintain a collection of microbes, which help to give the beer its "funk" factor. At first they wanted that factor to be lower because the public was not used to it, but as the beer gained popularity, they increased the funkiness during blending.

On the way home, Todd said that this style of wild beers could be the next wave of beers. He himself had been making them off and on through his brewing career, but always held back when he worked for someone else because he didn't want to contaminate their other beers with the bacteria and brettanomyces yeast required. Now he was excited to try them again—at home, at least.

"But I'd want to do a lot more research before ever starting an actual commercial brewery of my own," Todd said. "A *lot* more."

There was a quiet that settled in the car as we each thought our own thoughts.

"Well," I said finally. "Where should we go next, then?"

Todd turned and smiled. "You know, if we had unlimited amount of time and money, we could go to the Rare Barrel and Russian River in California, Jolly Pumpkin in Michigan, and Anchorage in Alaska, Crooked Stave in Colorado and... But, of course, we don't..."

I picked up the line: "There *is* one place where we can get the maximum bang for our buck if we're trying to learn more about starting up a brewery. Just as all marathon runners head for the Boston Marathon, all Elvis fans have Graceland on their bucket list, and all Muslims try to make the hajj to Mecca, we should go to Oregon."

And so we did.

❧ 10 ❧

The Oregon Iron Liver Tour

Three months later, a little jetlagged, we were sitting in a crowded, noisy brewery called Hair of the Dog in Portland, Oregon, at the ninth annual Fredfest. It was a gathering of brewers and drinkers to honor the legendary local and national beer writer Fred Eckhardt, but also to raise money for guide dogs for the blind, an international medical corps, and a brewing scholarship. On tap were twenty-five beers from all over the Northwest. For sixty dollars, attendees could eat all the food and drink all the beer they wished. The menu cover had a photoshopped image of a cloak-clad, light-saber wielding, cherubic 88-year old Fred with the inscription, "May the 4th be with you! From Fredi-Wan Kenobi."

Neither Todd nor I knew anyone, but that didn't make any difference. It was a friendly crowd, fueled by beers like BridgePort Brewing's Old Knucklehead, Ecliptic Brewing's Arcturus IPA, Logdson Farmhouse Ale's Tripple Straffe Drieling, and other IPAs and wild and funky beers. You didn't see these in Vermont, except in a beer store when they were travel-worn. We struck up a conversation with a couple who had come down from Seattle with their bicycles on Amtrak just for this event. "Seattle has good beer, but nothing like Portland," said the husband.

Alan Sprints, the owner of Hair of the Dog, was a welcoming fellow with a scraggly beard who looked more like a graduate student than a brewer. He invited us into the back brewery floor, for blessed quiet and a quick tour of his operation. While we sipped some of his Beer Week (a strong pale lager), he led us through his brewing tanks and his barrel room. There must have been over one hundred barrels in that room, stacked three high. It felt like a wine cellar. Alan had never brewed more than 800 barrels a year, but he said he could sell the beer for upwards of $300 a case. That was a size he could manage comfortably with only himself and an assistant, brewing ever-more complex beers.

Alan was very much influenced by Belgian beers and Belgian cooking. He was proud to be one of the first breweries to specialize in high-alcohol, bottle-conditioned beers which aged in barrels from six months to eight years. He tried to buy all the ingredients from an area within 350 miles of the brewery. The original brewing equipment was recycled from other industries and was still in use. He had a "library" of almost all of the beers he had made over twenty years. Meanwhile, the restaurant, bar and merchandizing brought in about 50 percent of his income. He sold beer to only two restaurants in Portland.

Our next stop was Upright Brewing. We almost missed it. Google maps took us to a non-descript office building and left us there with no signs—only a street filled with fancy-clad people headed to Kentucky Derby parties. One couple took pity on us and directed us to the basement.

Modest but functional. That was Upright. The brewery was open only two afternoons a week. Behind their door was no food, no music, no TV, only small groups of people sitting and sipping at small tables, talking in earnest tones. Todd poked me and said we could have been in France or Belgium. I felt it was like stopping at a country brewery in the Czech Republic. We were surrounded by wine barrels filled with beer flavored with all kinds of fruits: cherries, kumquats, persimmons, and peaches. Through a picture window, an open fermentation was at work. On the Upright website, they likened their beer to the complexity of jazz. *"At Upright the recipes and processes are decidedly unbound, making for true hybrid styles that share Charles Mingus' spirit of exercising creativity and craft."* After trying four of their beers, Todd and I smiled and pronounced this a true statement.

They sold a little beer there, but it was shipped out of Portland because the competition in the city was so fierce. It was the vibes of that place that made it unique. Todd said this was something he could imagine doing—selling wild beers once a week in an industrial setting.

What a contrast was our next stop, the Cascade Brewing Barrel

House, about two miles away. The scene reminded me of the Hofbräu-haus in Munich. It was a boisterous place with big screen TVs showing baseball. The crowd looked like a fraternity party better attuned to Corona or Pabst Blue Ribbon than to Kriek. They had almost twenty taps with nothing but sour beers with wonderful names like "Vlad the Imp Aler," "Regina," and "Marzipan."

Brewmaster Ron Gansberg said he made fruit wines and honey meads as a teenager before becoming a winemaker and then a brewer. He's been at it for twenty-five years. In over 1,400 French oak, bourbon, and wine barrels Gansberg and his crew age their browns, wheats, blonds, and porters, even nicknaming their brewing the House of Sour. They pushed the envelope of flavors and names. Innocently, Todd asked the woman at the bar, "How's the stout?" She looked at him as if he had two heads. "We don't DO stouts!"

Driving up the Columbia River to Hood River, we stopped at Pfriem Family Brewers, which was literally in the shadow of giant Full Sail Brewing Company. They were happy because Josh Pfriem had just been named Northwest "Brewer of the Year." The head brewer at Pfriem, Dan Peterson, had worked for Todd at Magic Hat.

The Pfriem Family had a real "bring it on" attitude. They liked the way brewers were pushing each other to do better in a friendly, competitive way. They said, "If our beer isn't good, it's our fault." In 2008, Josh and his wife traveled through Belgium on bikes. They studied beers from each region for a week. They especially liked the beers from Pajottenland where Lambic beer is produced. They loved the area so much they named their son Watou after a village in the province of West Flanders. When we were at their brewery, they were just installing two 45-hectoliter foeder vessels for their mixed culture fermentation projects.

About an hour out of Hood River, we got even closer to Belgium at Logsdon Organic Farmhouse Ales—a genuine farmhouse brewery with various animals milling around, including a small herd of Scottish Highlanders and a million-dollar view of Mount Hood thirty miles away. We sipped glasses of Cerasus, a beer that had recently won a gold medal for Belgian-style ale at the World Beer Cup contest. The owner of Logsdon is Oregon brewing legend Dave Logsdon, a founder of Full Sail Brewery and of Wyeast labs. Twenty-five years into running Wyeast, Logsdon grew tired of telling other people how to brew great beer with yeasts from his lab. He decided to develop a new palette of yeasts for his own brewery by traveling extensively in Europe.

As he told a reporter for *The Oregonian* in March 2013, "I isolated a handful of yeast strains I hadn't worked with before and started building a new collection. I knew I had the know-how to avoid the mutations and contaminations that become more common when combining multiple yeasts in a single beer. By combining yeasts, we could create a broader and fuller flavor profile, and it's really all about flavor." This experience resonated with Todd, who had begun to do something similar at home.

Logsdon Ales won numerous awards for their "Peche 'n Brett," and their "Seizen Bretta," using brettanomyces yeast. They have limited themselves to about 300 barrels a year due to location. Over the next several years they hope for nice slow growth. They plan to install a barrel room, a barrel cave, and a coolship. They'll also install oak foeders in the cave dug out of a nearby hill. Through Dave's wife, Judith, who is Belgian, they brought several graftings of Schaerbeek cherry trees to make a kriek-lambic style beer that would be spontaneously fermented. They said that the biggest challenge in the beginning was getting the bottle-conditioning right. They use locally sourced pear juice as opposed to sugar.

"What IS brettanomyces, anyway?" I asked Todd as we left and headed for Eugene.

"Brett is a wild yeast unlike standard brewing yeast; it's found blowing in the wind all over the world. When Brett is added or used right in brewing, it can contribute wonderful character to the finished beer. The flavors can be of cherry, pineapple, or citrus notes. But it can also add unpleasant, funky flavors, too, like fecal and plastic. But now there is big rush among brewers to use Brett. It's key to those Belgian, lambics, Flanders red ales, Gueuzes, Krieks, and Orvals. I think Orval showcases the classic Brettanomyces aroma and flavor. You really notice the difference when drinking young Orval at the brewery compared to a six-month-old from some beverage warehouse. Brett scavenges oxygen, breaks down dextrinous sugars, and changes the overall molecular structure of the beer. The resulting beer is tart and dry with an effervescent aroma of pineapple and citrus funk."

"So, the beer becomes a three-dimensional chess game of taste, color and tartness?"

"Yeah. Especially when you're blending different batches of beers."

In Eugene, we stopped off at Ninkasi Brewing, one of the fastest growing breweries in America. Todd's friend from Siebel, Head Brewer Mark Henion (who had lined up our visits across the state) gave us a tour of Ninkasi's massive equipment and state-of-the-art vessels. Standing amidst the 300-barrel fermenters, we felt we were in a hanger full of Saturn 5 fuel tanks. This was NOT Todd's dream job!

We finished the tour in a sensory tasting class with Bill Pengelly, the legendary ex-brewmaster from Deschutes, and Jamie Flood, one of the founders of Ninkasi. Jamie made an interesting comment about brewery competition. "There are twenty regional breweries and a thousand wannabes," he said. "A blood bath of breweries is coming. And if you grow, you may not be happy when you get there—even if you know where *there* is."

The contrast with our next stop was extreme. Paul Arney of Ale Apothecary looked like someone out of the '60s, with his goatee and a tie-dyed T-shirt. He presided over a one-person brewery next to his house in the woods ten miles outside Bend. The building could fit into a closet at Ninkasi.

Arney's father, grandfather, and great-grandfather were all independent drug store operators; when a customer came in, he or she had to trust the man across the counter. Arney's brewery was likewise small and transparent. When he worked at the pub at Deschutes, the customers were not interested in the labels on the beer; what they really wanted was to talk to the brewer and get to know what was happening behind the scenes and what made the beer the beer. Paul grew up in the sciences but grew to love to write and play music, which might have explained why he was attracted to brewing at a subconscious level.

Paul started at Deschutes in 1995. His work there led him "down a path of exploration. You learn and learn, and then you become a production brewer and you no longer have the creative outlet." The company promoted him to oversee ten other brewers. That is what the company needed, but Paul remembers just wanting to brew beer. "I decided to follow the beer and let it lead the way," he says. Once he started Ale Apothecary in 2011, he had no interest in the tap-handle rat race of pub distribution. He only wanted to do bottles. He wanted to mimic how Champagne is presented and take his beer to a new level. Since he couldn't afford to buy much new brewing equipment, he set up his space so that he does all his brewing or production out of wooden barrels. He welcomed the consumers who were pushing brewers to explore new things. As unorthodox as his brewery looks today, he believes this is the direction that breweries will go in the future. His current production was about 1,000 cases, or about 75 barrels.

On our drive back to Portland, I asked Todd: "So, what do you think?"

"This trip really brought Belgium to my mind—but in America. American wild ale is walking on the wild side! As Alan Newman says, there's always room for a great beer and what Gansberg and Logsdon and the others are doing proves it. These breweries are making money with a modest scale and investment. Instead of just doing the same old thing week after week, they are creating and pushing flavor into new beers all the time. These guys prove that beers can be drunk like wine. "What Paul Arney is doing really resonates with me. What a great intellectual brewer he is. He made a first-class beer and it sold itself."

"I confess," I said. "In the '90s, I gagged at hazelnut-flavored coffee and Magic Hat's #9 with its apricot flavor. Yuck! Now, with all the new and spiced and fresh fruited beers we've drunk out here, I've become a

Finally the limits of hoppiness is reached in a Vermont beer.

believer. I can appreciate experimental beers far, far out of the mainstream."

Todd became philosophical. "Ah, time just makes great things. With wild beers, you're letting a wonderful mix in nature evolve on its own terms. It's like letting artisanal cheese and other fermented products age at their own pace. That's the great thing about wild beers. You never know quite where they will go. Every beer is unique and we may never taste its like again.

"Unquestionably, you are taking a risk with wild beers. Doing traditional beers is stable, unchanging consistent. We've domesticated them. But with *wild* beers, you're giving some control back to the beer itself. That's why they're called wild! And what I've seen out here is that people *want* to try these new beers, and they want you to succeed because you're taking risks. People in Vermont would see that this is something different—a revolution in brewing."

I stared out the window at regal Mount Hood. Twenty years before, I had correctly gone "home to homebrew" from my sudsy professional dreams. But now that itch was back because of Todd's enthusiasm. Here was a guy who had never *left* homebrewing even as he became a professional brewer. He had taken busman's holidays in his basement throughout his professional career to experiment with other beers. Now he wanted to run between the legs of traditional brewers with his wild beers. The capital costs were low. We could experiment endlessly (at least until the money ran out). For me, it was a second chance to be an assistant brewer offering some awesome unusual beers to an excited public, and to do it without quitting my day job.

"What if we went in on this project together?" I blurted out. The words flowed like water through a burst dam. "I could put up half the money and you put up half and then throw in 98 percent of the intellectual property. We could do it on a small-enough scale to avoid banks. Twenty years ago, for a blessedly brief moment, I considered spending $250,000 on a stand-alone brewery, until I realized it was madness. But this? This is not mad. If it all goes smash or we can't meet our expenses after two or three years, we can shut it down and your kids can still go to college!"

Todd looked over at me. "Hmmmm. Interesting…"

⧉ 11 ⧉

Three Sips to Enlightenment

"'There are secrets in these barrels even I don't know.'"
—Rudi Ghequire, Brewmaster at Rodenbach

We went our separate ways for the rest of the summer, but several months after we got back from Oregon, I went out to Hinesburg to watch a soccer game at the high school where I had taught. Afterwards, I drove up to Todd's house on Texas Hill Road to talk about blenderies. There in the basement—surrounded by beer glasses, books, trays, posters, some beekeeping equipment, a cooler for beers and yeast strains— were twelve plastic carboys lined up around the wall like Grenadier Guards. Their liquids were a rainbow of colors with different substances (fruit, oak cubes, orange peels) floating on the top.

"Now this is impressive!" I said.

Todd picked up a flashlight and shined it into a few of the carboys. The carbon-dioxide bubbles in them rose like thousands of tiny helium-filled balloons. "It's been fun watching the beers progress, knowing that they are changing day by day, month by month. Regular yeast is tame and predictable, if handled correctly. It's like a dog. Wild yeast is like a cat, with a mind of its own." He snapped off the flashlight. "Of course, this isn't really the best test for these beers, but you can get close. Now, if they were aging in oak barrels, *that* would take it to a new level of complexity. That would be something!"

"It strikes me that brewing these kinds of beers is a bit like beekeeping," I said. I couldn't help but make the comparison. "We're working with live beings on the cusp between the domestic and the wild. With both, we are coaxing them to decide which course to take." With that, I took a yellow notepad out of my backpack. Back and forth, Todd and I went with ideas like ping pong balls. Ideas for a new blendery.

Our business plan was simplicity itself. Todd had the products in his mind, how he expected to make them and sell them, and how we would finance the first two years with our own money. It meant we didn't need to persuade anyone else—for example, a bank—with an elaborate business plan. However, a friend who teaches entrepreneurship suggested that although we didn't need a business plan for an operation of our size, it would be good to draw up a "working agreement." Thus, we cranked out the following clauses: Make complex and exciting beer on a small scale; Become the Vermont (or New England!) face of wild blendery beers; Educate consumers on what wild and funky beer can be ("Probiotic beer is good for you!"); Enjoy what we do and tell our story; Create our own distribution company; Build the brand slowly. Grow the business until it turns a profit; Work with chefs and other brewers and distillers on collaborative projects; Re-invest profits into the business (barrels, equipment, etc.); Have a hoppy funky *saison* as the main beer and roll out special blended barrels or fruited or vintage bottle releases as special events; Give ourselves two years to see where we are.

Long before we began to think about a blendery, Todd had been experimenting with fermented foods such as kimchi, kombucha, pickles, and sausages. At first, he had joked that the name of his own home should become "The House of Fermentology." Now that the blendery was in our sights, that name begged for legality...and fame. We submitted the application to the Vermont Secretary of State and for $20 became incorporated as "The House of Fermentology, LLC."

Meanwhile, what to call the beers themselves was harder to decide. How clever could we be? My first suggestion was to make a musical series based upon the number of ingredients—Solo, Duet, Trio, Quartet, Quintet, Sextet. Or we could build another type of musical series with Andante, Largo, Presto, Allegro, etc.

"Let's just keep it simple," replied Todd. "We'll put a different color dot on the shoulder of the bottle to represent the name of the beer and a matching label of the same color as the dot to identify the beer. In Belgium, that's how cellared beers were typically marked—with a paint swatch to represent the beer. It also has a connotation to the markings of a honeybee queen to designate her age. Plus, I haven't seen it before. The dot will be unique." In agreement, my son, Nick, suggested that "Simple Names, Complex Beers" could be a slogan.

Once we settled on that, we needed a place for our physical plant. Our needs were simple, but that didn't mean appropriate spaces were abundant. At first, Todd thought about putting the operation in his basement, which could hold eight or ten barrels. But that meant hauling the wort in from somewhere else up his steep hill. The clincher, of course, was that the feds don't allow a brewery in the living space of a house! We loved the idea of being in Burlington, with all its breweries and people, but all our real estate friends said forget about it. Too expensive and too scarce.

Todd drew up a list of space requirements. We needed an open-bay warehouse-style space with an overhead door, concrete floor and 500-1000 square feet with room to grow. We needed municipal water (hot water would be a bonus) and floor drains in the warehouse connected to a municipal sewer. This would be for washing barrels. We needed enough heat to keep temperature controlled during the winter. Finally, we need electrical connections of 120/208 volts for running our pumps.

Looking around the village of Hinesburg, the only place Todd could find immediately was next to a Baptist Church! On his way home from work, he began to make long detours around the county to view possible sites. He found some spots that were cheap, but far out of the way, other sites with everything but an overhead door. Still others had everything, but cost $20 a square foot in annual rent. Likes moths to a flame, we kept coming back to Pine Street in Burlington. It was surely more expensive than the hinterlands, but it was less than half a mile from both Switchback and my house. It was blooming with artists, small businesses, and two more breweries, Queen City and Zero Gravity. It was a main thoroughfare in and out of town. The city's first brewery, Petersen's, had been in this district. I was also partial to Pine Street because when I was in the legislature, I played a small role in founding the South End Business Association to expand the area as an arts and light industrial corridor. How much fun it would be to end up there with my own business!

After several weeks of searching, we stumbled upon a space at Noyes Automotive, a New England-wide tire store and repair shop right on Pine Street. I had been getting tires changed there for decades, and I never noticed their bays on a side street. Through the dusty windows, it looked, well, crowded. It was being rented by Ben and Jerry's to house their "assault vehicle" for the Occupy Wall Street movement. But when we got inside, it had just about everything we needed. The House of Fermentology thus became the fourth malt-based business within a quarter mile—Burlington's "beer belt!"

Of course, nothing is perfect. Our bay in the Noyes building held the central compressor for running all their hydraulic equipment. When it kicked on every fifteen minutes, you couldn't talk. Fortunately, each cycle ran for only a minute or two. There would also have be some repairs, like a concrete slab on half the floor and a fire-resistant wall, but this site was too good and convenient to miss. And, the price was reasonable.

For our discussions about the beers we would eventually brew in the space, we began meeting at Speeder & Earl's, a coffee shop on Pine Street not far from our noisy Noyes bay. In a former manufacturing space where the innocuous music and heating fan performed a white noise duet, we juiced our ideas on caffeine, not beer.

"Okay. So where are you getting the wild yeast for our beers?" I asked Todd.

"I've been developing a house culture for a year now. It's a mixed culture of several strains of Brett, lactic acid bacteria, and some ale yeast. I think we should keep the base beer lighter and less tart on the palate—like a field or table beer brewed in the saison style and aged in

117

French oak wine barrels. We don't need to brew to a specific style. After all, we're brewing American wild ales and we can grow our line of beers from that either by fruiting the beer or aging them in different barrel types like gin, cognac, or rum. Think of a Flemish red in a bourbon barrel or even an *Oud bruin* in a port barrel. The true experimentation will be how the beer develops over time in the barrel or bottle."

Todd reminded me that these beers' flavors would evolve over time, but we would have to accept the fact that some barrels might turn very negative in flavor. We would just have to say "bye-bye" and dump them. That is the nature of this beer. You try and control things as best you can, but it won't always go according to plan. Everything is a risk.

Risk aside, we decided that the saison would come out every three months once we built up an inventory of barrels with some age. Our selection would keep evolving and revolving. Every batch could be slightly different because every barrel has a life of it own, but that's where the blending process would come in. We could raise or lower the acidity, dry hop, or add fruit. We could offer an endless variety of beers because of the blending.

"And the flexibility of the brews is the main draw?" I asked. "Are we thus building a reputation for *predictable unpredictability?*"

"A little bit, sure. Every batch we bottle could be slightly different, but the direction will remain the same. The beer will let us know when it's ready."

Getting into the spirit of hyperbole, I riffed a little: "So our beer will be a Rubik's cube of complexity."

Todd preferred the analogy of jazz and *its* complexity. "People will understand beer as jazz, and you, the brewer, are Coltrane. The complexity of jazz means no performance is ever the same thing. The watchword is improvisation. You can always tell a good band. Even on its worst night, it's still good."

We started the process to apply for a federal Brewer's Notice with the Alcohol and Tobacco Tax and Trade Bureau (TTB) which would allow us to operate an alcohol-based business. It had questions about our possible criminal record, if any, sources of funds, power of attorney, etc. From the City of Burlington, we got our conditional zoning permit, and applied the crimson " Z" to the door of our bay for the required two weeks. Then we went down the street to the Public Works department, only 300 yards away from our space, for a building permit. And there began the biggest glitch of the whole process.

It turned out we didn't have fire-rated walls or a fire door separating us from the adjoining spaces. It took four months, with the help of an architect friend, and additional costs, to get the walls designed, built and approved.

In mid-October, just as the wall was being completed, our TTB notice came through on Todd's wedding anniversary. From that notice flowed directly the state manufacturing license and a fourth class liquor license, which would allow us to dispense small glasses for tasting or purchase, and take-away closed containers. Two weeks later, after an inspection by the State Liquor Control Board, we had our two state licenses, and we were ready to brew. All in all, we were seven months getting the paperwork and construction done.

While we were in the middle of planning the House of Fermentology, two brewers from Switchback asked to meet with Todd "off campus." They were Bobby Grim and Sam Keane. Todd had mentored them during their employment at Switchback. Sam came from a food science background. He and Todd worked together doing a study on Switchback beers with an intern from UVM. They developed the taste sensory program for Switchback brewery employees. Bobby worked with Todd to developed the pilot brewing system. They developed more than half of the new beers between 2012-2014.

In March, after Todd had told Bobby and Sam about our House of Fermentology venture, they told him that they were leaving Switchback to set up a small brewery. They wanted Todd to join them. According to Todd, it was a lot to absorb. He was already committed to HOF. He and Monica had a long talk about it; the opportunity was appealing. After reading the business plan, Todd and Monica were convinced that Bobby and Sam were serious and this was a great opportunity. Monica said Todd would regret it if he didn't go for it. And so began Foam Brewers—a new brewpub on the waterfront in Burlington.

The synergies with House of Fermentology were immediately apparent and desirable. With a seven-barrel system, Foam would be able to brew our wort as well as their own beer. Bobby and Sam wanted to have our sours on tap and for sale by bottle. We could do joint marketing with them.

At the "House" we could sell tastings of our sours and bottles for takeaway, and then say, "If you want the full experience of drinking our beer while eating good food, then go to Foam!" It would relieve us of the expense of prettifying our space. We could remain in the thick of the Pine Street brewery beer district and never be tempted to go into the pub business. We could even set up a joint distribution company.

Through these months of preparation, I kept pinching myself. I thought back to interviews with Jack McAuliffe, Fred Eckhardt, Fritz

Maytag and those other pioneers and how I had first dreamed of joining their fraternity until reality intervened. Now I was actually doing this by wedding my dreams to the hard ambition of a friend. The trip to Oregon sealed it for me, as I watched Todd become more and more enthused.

We began bringing in equipment even while the wall was being built. Compared to building a regular brewery, our equipment needs were few and inexpensive. No mash tun, no hot water tank, no kettle, no heat exchangers, no stainless steel fermenters, no grain mill, no bins for grain storage. We did, however, need barrels. We bought them in two batches. Shaun Hill put Todd in contact with Adam Crockett of Keystone Fermentation. Adam procures barrels for brewers on the East Coast from Europe in large format wood tanks. All our barrels are French oak and although they have wonderful aromas, they are neutral in flavor.

As Todd explained, "Wine makers typically retire their barrels after a few aging cycles because they become neutral in flavor or lose the tannins and sugars in the wood. For our purpose, that's not a problem. We don't want the tannin, so these barrels are just right for us. For all that a winemaker does to keep Brettanomyces yeast *out* of the winery, we will be putting it *into* the barrels. We will want a host of positive micro-organisms living in our barrels."

In addition to our 225-liter (59-gallon) wine barrels, we bought a 25-hectoliter (21-barrel) oak tank and a used 7-barrel Grundy tank that would be used for bottling. Matt Cohen from Fiddlehead donated a tank from his equipment boneyard to round out our tank and barrel needs. Our plan was to brew batches of wort at a partner brewery and then haul them in two 330-gallon totes from Citizen Cider in a rented truck to HOF. That would make about 20-barrel brews.

Even before the barrels arrived, we bought a pallet jack with a 1-ton capacity for moving equipment around. The last piece of the puzzle was our packaging equipment. Our timing was just right because Mystic Brewing Company in Chelsea, Massachusetts, was upgrading their bottling equipment. We were able to purchase his gravity bottle-filler and Champagne-style corker. He threw in the bottle rinser and carbon-dioxide bottle purge setup, too. Along with a list of other miscellaneous needs and a pump for moving wort and beer around from totes to tanks to barrels and bottles, this completed our equipment list.

Our next task was to find a symbol for our House of Fermentology. I was determined to have something simple. For years I had obsessed over the Bass Ale red triangle in Manet's painting, *A Bar at the Folies Bergere*. I loved Shaun Hill's Hill Farmstead mirror image of beer glasses. Locally, I liked the style of artist Clark Derbes, whose work oscillated from two to three dimensions in paint and wood. It was a mixture of op art and M.C. Escher. Coincidentally, his studio was next door to the Noyes building. For a small fee, he agreed to do a few drafts. We suggested that he add some Brett yeast cells as smoke coming from the chimney, and *voila!* We had a design so handsome and so clean that we hired him to paint a giant version on the HOF wall. That same "house" became central to our entire image, and central to our intellectual property.

But ultimately, all the preparations for our House will be secondary to the beer itself. With Todd and me, American-style wild beer has found true advocates, real devotees—and our mission is to proselytize. Wild beer enthusiasts sometimes gush about how the style helped to launch a "winification of beer." First off, the beer's complexity lends itself to pairings with different kinds of food. To prove this thesis, one evening I joined Todd and Monica for some test-pairings of wild ales with different cheeses. We set out a tray of bries, blues, goat cheeses, and something with a funky washed rind, and served them up with crackers and fig jam. We uncapped some 375-ml bottles of Todd's wild ale and watched the carbon-dioxide snake out of the bottles. We cupped the smell. Ah, it was ambrosia!

Moreover, we do believe you have to slow down and sip it. Given the distinctiveness of this beer, I wondered if we may need to teach our new customers how to drink and appreciate it. Todd suggested we encourage people to cast away their thoughts of what beer is, and re-think what beer *could* be. "In a way," he said, "it's like when you tried your first serious IPA. It probably blew your head off!" This beer is even more untamed than a heady IPA; it's wild. It's sour, tart, filled of malic acid twang, and yet, ultimately, it's pleasant, wonderfully refreshing, and very complex. The variations are endless with different malts, hops, yeasts, carbonation, fruits, and bacteria. For thoughtful drinkers, it will be like going into a house of mirrors. The sensations go on and on, and double back on themselves.

According to Todd, you need three sips to enlightenment. The first taste is filled with the shock of something really new, and the taste ricochets around your palate like a particle in a cyclotron. Your palate simply has to adjust. The second sip gets the saliva moving, and you begin to taste the other flavors: the fruit, the spices. Your taste buds adapt and they ask for more. The third sip gives you a chance to savor the big complexity of the beer and open your mind to what beer can be in the future. You will never think of beer the same way again. *It's the power of sour!* The more complex our beers are, the more people will savor them. That's where blending comes in.

Throughout this adventure, the image of Todd as composer-conductor has come repeatedly to my mind. With every batch of HOF beers and flavors, he will create and orchestrate new pieces. I remember him quoting Miles Davis: "It's not the notes you play, it's the notes you don't play." As I move from homebrewing into the House of Fermentology, my excitement of thirty years ago has returned. This "making beer" journey—for the two of us now—has been a treat at every turn (for the notes we played, and didn't play). And so has the beer. We believe you will think so, too.

Stop, sip, and savor!

Acknowledgments

We would like to thank the following people for their help and encouragement with the making of this book: Chris Hadsel, Emily Copeland, Jeff Danziger, Paul Arney, John Kimmich, Robert Grim, Sam Keane, Clark Derbes, Taylor Johnson, Jon Farmer, Eliza DuPont, Justin McCarthy, Bob McKearin, Staige Davis, Paul Sayler, Matt Cohen, Ella Haire, and Neika Haire.

CPSIA information can be obtained
at www.ICGtesting.com
Printed in the USA
BVOW06s0904090417
480735BV00012B/236/P